The
Psalms of Prayer

Secrets on how to use the Book of Psalms to increase the
Power of your Prayers!

• • • • • • • • • • • • • • • • •

Madam Oracle

The Guarded Psalms of Prayer

Secrets on how to use the Book of Psalms to increase the Power of your Prayers!

Spiritually Fit Publications
581 N. Park Ave. Ste. #725
Apopka, FL 32704
MadamO@MadamOracle.com

Published in the United States of America
ISBN-13: 978-1532724527
$14.95

Table of Contents

DEDICATION

I dedicate this book to my Lord and Savior, who is first and foremost in my life. I thank Him for the love, as well as the information that He has poured into the depths of my soul to ensure that I am able to bless the lives of many. It has taken a lot of rejection, hurt, betrayal, and pain to get *"The Guarded Psalms of Prayer"* out of me, and I pray that it brings bountiful blessings in your life and the lives of others.

I would like to give a great big THANK YOU to everyone who contributed to or played their role in my life that led up to *"The Guarded Psalms of Prayer."* Every experience has provided a valuable lesson that I would not have received otherwise or would have overlooked; therefore, I am very thankful and grateful. But I would also like to give a special thank you to a very young man who OPENED my eyes to what's really taking place in the real world regarding the games people play. I was an open book for new information, I soaked it up, and now

I am activating the Law of Reciprocity, giving it back to you in the Spirit of LOVE.

I am so happy that I did not give up on love—loving God, loving myself, and loving others unconditionally. And, due to my unchangeable, loving and giving heart, God's grace and mercy gave me a promise that "The last shall be first, and the first, shall be last." He also spoke into my heart that "My latter days would be greater than my former days, and it will come to pass." That was my promise, and that was the hope that rested in my heart with my unshakeable faith regardless of whether I felt loved or unloved by others—the love of God and the love of myself superseded all else because I was on a mission. A mission to love people and build the lives of others one at a time, even if they did not care about me, it was my reasonable service to lead the way in LOVE regardless of how I felt. I accepted being mistreated like a champ because I had to learn, understand, and share the lessons behind the actions with the world. I was called to put my **Oracle-ism Spin** on this one thing that we take for granted, and that is LOVE. Although my perspective is a little different, but it works in ways that only the human psyche will respond.

If we've had love all our lives, then we do not know what it's like to go through life being truly unloved. Therefore, we take it for granted, becoming selfish and unreasonable to those who fall out of our circle of love......is this fair? Absolutely not! However, one is not able to see that because they really do not know what it feels like to go through life with a smile on their face, knowing that the only person that's really on their side is GOD. And, for this reason, I share *"The Guarded Psalms of Prayer"* to ensure that everyone will have an equal opportunity to love and be loved effectively.

INTRODUCTION

Having an ITCH that you cannot scratch is one of the worst feelings that you could ever experience. However, when it comes down to having an ITCH from within, then what do you do? This book reveals the secrets of how to deal with mental, physical, spiritual, emotional and mental woes to ensure that you get exactly what you want, need, and deserve out of life.

Applying *"The Guarded Psalms of Prayer"* is the best way to gain control over our lives, and to learn the difference between our perception and our reality. We will always find ourselves talking about living a great life, but why do we often make it such a hard task when it's just a choice away, or better yet, one prayer away? As a matter of fact, if we take a moment to reflect on our past choices, we will find that it has been our perception and the lack of prayer that has caused the most problems in our lives, opposed to the people, places, and things around us. I know about this all too well, and it's my reasonable service to share *"The Guarded Psalms of Prayer"* that has brought me to my present state of mind.

Like many, I speak and pray to God every day; I express the desires of my heart and the lack thereof. I also give thanks in all things, the good, and the not so good as well. But, more importantly, I ask God every morning to allow me to become a blessing to others; therefore, He gives me wisdom, hope and the motivation to inspire others as well as myself. My greatest gift is the ability to motivate and encourage others through whatever I'm dealing with, going through, growing through, or praying through.

I walk in my destiny every day by finding ways to encourage or spark greatness within everyone I come in contact with. My mission is to enhance the lives of others one at a time, as well as to enhance my own life every single day. I look for ways to learn something new; actually, it's like an expectation for me—I expect nothing less than learning more than I did the day before while discarding the things that I do not need. It is imperative for me to cleanse my mind of all the unwanted things that have the potential to shift my way of thinking or have the potential to clutter my mind with unfruitful thoughts. Although, some may think that I am a little insensitive when it comes down to my thoughts; however, I believe that it's through our thoughts that an action is taken—so, any thought that produces a negative reaction within me, I will discard if there is not a lesson for me to learn.

Am I perfect? Absolutely not! I have issues, strengths, and weaknesses like everyone else—I just make it my business to focus 80% of my time on my strengths, and 20% of my time to work on my weaknesses without passing judgment. I assume total responsibility for myself, my life, my dreams, my goals, and my mishaps in life. I know exactly what I want and do not want, so it's my responsibility to get what I want and get rid of what I do not want. I have found that most of us settle for less than what we deserve due to our impatience—we are in a right now world and we must get what we want right now. I have found that the right now satisfaction is not always the best. We need time to think and pray about what we are doing before we engage in it, because a rushed decision may incorporate our deepest regrets. Now I present to you, *"The Guarded Psalms of Prayer."*

CHAPTER 1
Guarded From Within

Why do we do what we do? Or, better yet, why do we not love the way we should love? The "why's" of life gives us an opportunity to understand ourselves when we are misunderstood regarding what we are or are not doing, what we are or are not saying, what we are or are not becoming, or who we are or are not loving. Love and Freedom are all around us; we cannot get away from them. But the question remains, "Why does love or the lack of freedom hurt so badly?" "Why does love or the lack of freedom deceive us?" "Why does love and bondage break our heart?" Why, Why, Why, Why…..Can someone really answer these questions? The answer is "Yes." That someone is Y.O.U. Yes, that is correct; you are the only one that can truly answer the

"Why's" of your Version of Love and Freedom. By not answering this one question, it creates an ITCH from within the depths of your soul. Because where there is a lack of love, there will always be a lack of freedom mentally, physically, emotionally, or spiritually.

By simply asking fact-finding questions of purpose and taking the time to understand the what's, when's, where's, how's, and why's of love and freedom, we then get the precious privilege of opening the gate to the Fountain of Wisdom that's buried within the depths of our very own soul. Yes, we have the answers within us, and all we have to do is seek the answers from within opposed to getting the superficial opinions from people who are not connected to our soul. I am not saying that receiving advice is wrong—I am saying that the advice that one receives from someone else should bring confirmation to the answers that we receive from within. Therefore, we have less time to focus on being judged or judging others on what we may be guilty of ourselves or what we have hidden in our past repertoire of secrets that are filed under a different label according to our level of blindness or our perception of our reality.

Through this book entitled, *"The Guarded Psalms of Prayer,"* I can definitely give you my version of the "What's," "How's," "When's," and "Where's" of LOVE and FREEDOM to ensure that you are able to fill in the blanks of your life. However, as life would have it, the Plan of God is not set in stone for anyone—He did not create robots, nor will He violate your FREE WILL!

Everyone is different, and everyone will have their own path in life. And, for that reason, you have options, choices, lessons, and repercussions that will define the chapters of your life regardless of whether you desire for them to do so or not.

Throughout my journey in life, I have found that LOVE is the foundation to all things, and when we lack love or become cold-hearted, we will lose our way in life. The opposite of love is evil, and if you read evil backward, it tells you to "LIVE!" They are all connected, and if we are not exhibiting love, then what are we exhibiting? There is no in-between on this one! Whether we exhibit love or evil, they affect how we live; therefore, one must become very cognizant of his or her actions, reactions, thoughts, and desires on a moment-by-moment basis to ensure that the coldness of life does not create a heart of ice or a bed of waywardness.

King Solomon in the Bible put together several proverbs to guide us in practical wisdom regarding life skills to safeguard our blessings, to prevent us from cursing our own hand, and to bring structure into our lives. As his legacy lives on, the same wisdom that he asked for, is available to each and every one of us, we only need to ask and follow instructions. The Voice of Wisdom says in Proverbs 8:1-4, *"Does not wisdom cry out, And understanding lift up her voice? She takes her stand on the top of the high hill, beside the way, where the paths meet. She cries out by the gates, at the entry of the city, at the entrance of the doors: "To you, O men, I call."* It doesn't matter how we may or may not feel about reading the Bible, but there are indeed hidden truths that ungodly individuals have mastered to outsmart Godly individuals. I am not here to judge who exhibits Godly characteristics and who does not, my goal is to empower willing vessels with vital lifesaving information. Now, with that in mind, our "Why's" in life are directly linked to our emotions, and if we do not learn how to heal or deal with our emotional self, it definitely will become hard to deal with someone else's Version of Love. Although we all have our own perception of love, but there are rules, strategies, guidelines, and concepts to love that one must uncover to be able to love God, love self, and love others as if one has never been hurt before; if not, we are destined to become enslave by something or someone that creates a form of bondage for us.

As life progresses with or without us, the wisdom and love that I have put into *"The Guarded Psalms of Prayer"* has an insurmountable treasure chest of benefits that are designed to teach us the SPIRITUAL way of getting what we want without creating enemies along the way. Here are some of the learnable benefits that are available to you in this book:

- Learn how to love effectively.
- Learn the fear of God.
- Learn the value of love with everyone.
- Learn wisdom and discipline.

- Learn the value of understanding.
- Learn how to receive and obey instructions.
- Learn how to deal with life lessons.
- Learn how to value knowledge.
- Learn how to exercise discretion.
- Learn why we need to exercise prudence.
- Learn how to embrace wise counsel.
- Learn how to treat people.
- Learn the value of respect.
- Learn the importance of humility.
- Learn who to hang out with or who to avoid.
- Learn how to develop Godly character.
- Learn how to treat your parents or your elders.
- Learn about the rod of correction.
- Learn how to break free of any form of bondage,

"The Guarded Psalms of Prayer" brings the GOOD NEWS and GOOD TIDINGS of LOVE to all who are willing to receive it on a SILVER PLATTER. Now it is your time to take a moment to look within for the answers to life most mind-boggling questions about why you are doing what you are doing or why you are not doing what you should be doing. Inner wisdom awaits your quest for the answers to your "Why's" in life.

In a world where heroes, champions, role models, and idols are created, there are a vast amount of people who are really great, but do not realize it. Their mind, body, soul, and spirit are consumed with an ITCH that they haven't a clue on how to scratch; therefore, they find themselves filling in the blanks of their life as they go along.

An ITCH from within is basically a longing that we all have, some more than others, but we all have a longing from within for something or someone. An inner ITCH can also be referred to as an inner struggle, spiritual warfare, vexed spirit, or longing. The difference is that some people understand that they need help and that they need to work on themselves every single day, and some could care less about inner growth. However, with an ITCH that is not scratched or soothed, we will find that the ITCH becomes much stronger causing us to settle for people, places, and things that we are not happy with.

Life as we would call it, has a structural connection to everything and everyone that we hold dear to us. Our past creates an element of our present struggles from within; that controls our present and future actions, reactions, attitudes, and demeanor; therefore, determining our level of greatness or ITCH from within. For example, the people with the worst attitudes are usually the ones with the biggest ITCH. Although we have all suffered some form of known or unknown abuse; however, the ones with the biggest ITCH are usually the ones who are in the most denial.

A person with an ITCH from within is most often depressed and/or stressed all the time. We will also find that their self-worth is so damaged that their self-esteem drops to an all-time low, subjecting them to abuse in many forms. Whether they are the abuser or the abusee, there are 7 main reasons why an individual abuse others or tolerate abuse:

1. Loneliness
2. Anger
3. Insecurity
4. Low self-esteem
5. Conditioning
6. Helplessness
7. Broken heart

An unknown author once said, "Anger is one letter short of danger." I personally, stay away from individuals who are angry all the time. For me, it's like a time bomb waiting to happen. Actually, most people only think of abuse as being physical in nature; however, there are many different forms of abuse that contribute to an irritating ITCH of an abuser, and his or her victims. Let's just talk about the different forms of abuse:

Physical Abuse – Begins with physical contact that causes bodily harm to another, such as beating, pushing, punching, slapping, pinching, choking, snatching, etc. This is by far the most familiar form of abuse, as well as the most recognizable, and judged form; however, with physical abuse, we are able to heal; but with the other forms of abuse that come with it, may last a lifetime. However, the discipline of a child and physical abuse are totally different; as long as bodily harm is not caused, discipline is coming out of love, and the child has an understanding of why discipline is necessary. Anything other than that, or outright abusing someone to control them is always attached to mental or emotional abuse; therefore, creating a double-edged sword of resolvable issues that must be dealt with accordingly.

Mental Abuse – Begins with bullying, intimidating, or creating a hostile environment to brainwash someone. Most often this is accomplished by making the abusee think that they are crazy, or that they are at fault for the situation, circumstance, or event. A mentally abusive person may also make threats to hurt or kill themselves, the person's family, friends, to ruin a person financially, to destroy personal property, spread gossip, or to reveal a person's innermost secrets through mind-games. Although mind control takes a little longer to accomplish; but, it has the most profound impact that goes unrecognized by the abusee. However, a mentally abused person is most recognized by their actions, reactions, thoughts, beliefs, and fears; therefore, having the double-impact as an abuser, and the abusee to say the least. In so many words, a mentally abused person is destined to knowingly or unknowingly become an abuser if they do not receive some sort of intervention.

Emotional Abuse – Begins with verbal abuse, such as name-calling, criticizing, belittling, embarrassment, manipulation, coercion, ignoring, or extreme humiliation. This may also include the deprivation of affection, deprivation of attention, deprivation of approval, bullying, or outright rejection. This often occurs when the abuser refuses to accept responsibility for anything, and finds fault in the abusee to make himself or herself feel superior, that they cannot do anything wrong, or they are justified in their actions. I have found that emotional abuse also occurs, when the abuser goes out of their way to make an individual feel rejected or unwanted. Most often with emotional abuse, the abuser knows exactly what they are doing, because they have to make a conscious effort to think of things to reject, manipulate, coerce, hurt, or bring harm to the abusee. Defamation of character is definitely a thought-out behavior that sets Karma in motion faster than any other form of abuse.

Spiritual Abuse – Begins when a person uses the Bible to manipulate others, to control others, or using scripture to justify his or her actions through misrepresentation. This also may incorporate the use of negativity, or causing ill-will through bad-mouthing, negative prayers, or negative thinking of those who do not know what they are doing. However, for those who could care less about what they are doing often use prayers, rituals, or spells to control others, through the use of Black Magic, Wicca, Voodoo/Hoodoo, Santeria, etc. Although, we may not talk about Spiritual Abuse much, or deny the use of such practices; but, there is a reason why the Spiritualist/Fortune Teller/Occultist stay in business, and most often, it is through our ignorance, greed, or selfishness. This type of behavior has been around since the beginning of time, and it is not going anywhere; therefore, we must learn how to equip ourselves for Spiritual Warfare, because we do not wrestle against flesh and blood, but against principalities, against powers, against the rulers of darkness in high places.

Economic Abuse – Begins when a person uses money as a form of punishment, or when an individual makes his or her partner beg for basic necessities. It could fall under overspending as well; however, extreme abuse in this area comes about when a person demands that his or her partner gives them their whole paycheck, spending the whole paycheck on wayward activities, or who counts the money down to the exact penny. This also includes keeping a mate from seeking employment, or making them suffer financially so that they can depend on them.

Sexual Abuse – Begins when an individual is forced to have sex or indulge in explicit behavior that degrades them. This is also applicable to being treated like a sex object, solicited for sex, withholding sex, or accusations of affairs. In today's time, this is most often used in open relationships, controlled relationships, or the friends with benefits relationships. We have gotten to the point that sexual abuse has become second-nature, especially when men and women are giving themselves away for power, money, and status. It is often said that everyone has a price, which is true to a certain extent, because we are mere flesh and blood; but, why would we abuse someone to the point where they would have to choose to be abused because of money, power, or status?

The one thing that I have found is that abuse occurs in every culture and in every socioeconomic level. Regardless of where we are in life, we will think 1 of 4 things:

1. We will think that abuse will never happen to us.
2. We will think that we deserve to be abused.
3. We will think that we **do not** deserve to be abused.
4. We will think that we have the right to abuse.

Most often, we believe that women are more abused than men; however, I beg to differ on that. Men are just as abused as women; they just do not mention it because they are experts at keeping secrets. Actually, men are more susceptible to all forms of abuse except for physical abuse. It is indeed true that more women are prone to physical abuse than men, but with all the other forms of abuse, men rank just as high, if not higher. Of course, men are not going to mention that they are being emotionally abused, mentally abused, economically abused, sexually deprived/manipulated, or being stalked by their wives or girlfriends! Whether it's male or female, abuse is all around us, in our homes, hostile environments in the workplace and in our social endeavors as well. The writing is always on the wall with an abuser or an abusee—so if we can't get away from it, we must learn and understand it to ensure that we do not become the next victim.

The ultimate goal of an abuser is to seek power and precedence over something or someone. The love of power and the fear of losing it will drive an abuser to great extremes. Here are a few things that we need to know:

1. The pains of the past produce our problems of today.

2. The victim as a child often grows up to be victimized as an adult.

3. Abuse victims often become a perfectionist and high achievers.

4. Those who are often abused become abusers.

5. Abuse victims feel they are to blame.

6. Headaches, asthma, body pain, eating disorders are often symptoms of abuse or emotional problems.

7. Abusers are often respected people.

8. Angry people sometimes blame others for their misfortunes.

9. A negative self-image stems from real or perceived deprivation or rejection as well as abuse.

10. Sexual abuse often leads to sexual problems, promiscuity, or secret acts of prostitution.

11. Suppressed emotions often lead to physical symptoms.

12. Forgiveness is essential for emotional healing.

Abuse is unacceptable, regardless of what type it is. Whether we are married, unmarried or anything in between, when there is an ITCH from within, we will often ask ourselves:

1. What's wrong with me?
2. What have I done so wrong?
3. Why do I keep attracting these types of relationships?
4. Will I ever meet the right person?

Our conditioning or programming from our childhood experiences determine the level of anger we exhibit, our level of self-esteem, as well as our level of security. They amazingly work together regardless of whether we were raised by both parents, neglected by a parent, mistreated by a parent, lost a parent during childhood, abandoned, or whether we had surrogate parents or raised by an institution—positive and negative programming will take place. For the individuals whose parents were physically or emotionally absent, rest assured that there will be self-esteem issues of unworthiness, unlovability, or insecurity that needs to be worked on or worked at on a consistent basis. When dealing with these types of issues, we very well may spend years unlearning, relearning or getting over some things, but we must truly understand the point of origin if we want to really understand who we are as a person, and why we are as an individual.

I have found that negative experiences and hurt produces baggage; and, with every piece of baggage, the ITCH gets stronger and more frequent. Therefore, we must find a way to refuse the baggage that we do not want to keep. Improving ourselves is at its best when we are able to see beyond the negative to get to the positive. We are in control over our lives and having a positive attitude will definitely give us the upper-hand in doing so. However, when we feel as if we are in control, we will always feel a sense of wanting or achieving more, which is only natural for us. As a matter of fact, we all want more time in the day, but if we had it what would we do? Would we accomplish more, waste more time, watch more TV, find more unproductive things to cram into our time? We all want more money, but if we had it what would we do? Would we save it, invest it, buy more stuff, accrue more bills, help others, etc. We all want more of something; and for that reason, we need to know what we are going to do with the things that we are hoping and praying for.

It is okay to want and to become more; but, we must ensure that a positive change occurs within our mind first. If not, we will find ourselves wanting people, places, and things for the wrong reasons. Besides, when we are able to deal with the negativity in our lives, we are better able to make wise decisions while developing great strategies on how to turn a superficial negative into a positive.

You will always have the potential to make your dream or passion happen as long as you do not give up on yourself. My friend, when you learn how to pray effectively, while using scripture to back it up, you will then position yourself to become strong emotionally; as a result, you are better able to deal with the negativity that surrounds you. You are the best positive you that you have, so make the most of it. Of course, I know that you hear about this positive hoopla all the time; and I write as if it's so easy. I know personally that it's not always easy; especially when you are going through something; but the freedom of love will change everything if we believe.

Prayer

Father, My God in the Name of Jesus, I pray that on this day that You bless me to be a blessing to myself and others. Lord, I also pray that You help me to love myself, and love others the way You love, with no strings attached. Moreover, if I have found favor in Your sight, please allow Your Divine Love to flow through my veins to ensure that Your Divine Love is freely pumped into the lives of others. My God, I have found that Your love has become a lamp under my feet and a light unto my path; therefore, when people see me, they will also see a representation of Your love as well.

When I feel the sting of hurt or rejection, allow it to bounce off me as if nothing happened. And, for this reason, I ask in the Mighty Name of Jesus, that You strengthen my heart to deal with the emotional woes of life. Although, I may not receive love in return from others, but I know that Your grace is sufficient enough where I will not feel the sting of rejection. Father, as love has no boundaries in my heart; therefore, I ask that you grant me the wisdom on how to use love, how to share love, when to share love, where to share love, the reasons why I am sharing my love with others, and the inspiration to do so.

My Father, in the midst of extending my genuine love for myself, and others—let me not become prey to those who are callus at heart, or the vultures by nature. I also pray, in the Name of Jesus, that You cover me from the abusers, manipulators, or the wayward individuals who have a desire to intentionally or unintentionally crush me. Father, as You cleanse and purify my mind, body, soul, and spirit of the limitations that will hinder my walk with You—I declare and decree that You open the flow of love in and out of my life, availing Your grace and mercy on high. For this, O' Lord, I give thanks to You, and Your praises will be continually on my lips. Amen.

Scripture Reading:

Psalms 8
Psalms 10
Psalms 37

CHAPTER 2

Guarded Emotions

As we continue to breathe the breath of life, emotions will flow through our veins whether we like it or not. Our emotions are a vital part of our being that we try to block out. It is through the blocking of our emotions that cause us the greatest pain and losses in life. In order to truly embrace the essence of blissful living, we must understand and respect our emotions; if not, we will find ourselves emotionally bound. If we take a moment to look around us, we will find that everyone is trying to knowingly or unknowingly fill a void from within—we are created that way.

Avoid that's ignored will cause the best of us to start looking for love in all the wrong places, going overboard to please others or simply trying too hard to make someone love us. Although everyone will have his or her own set of issues to deal with; however, when we have the facts about why we are doing what we do, we are better able to find the solution. *Nevertheless, throughout my many years of meeting great people, I met this beautiful young lady named Kinsey. She was absolutely gorgeous. After speaking with her for several hours, I found that this beautiful woman was the most insecure woman I have ever met. She constantly criticized herself, her abilities, and her life. I could not believe that such a phenomenal woman could be so negative and that she hated the life that God has so gracefully blessed her with.*

After expressing sincere compassion for Kinsey, she began to open up to me—she explained how she was born as a result of an affair. She went on to tell me how her mother had a serious crush on this married guy, and the only way to keep this man in her life was to get pregnant—so she did. She gave birth to Kinsey, and her father kept it a secret from his wife for about 7 years. Kinsey's mom got tired of waiting for him to leave his wife, so she decided to break up his home by telling his wife about the affair and his secret child. The wife and Kinsey's mom got into a big fight—they pulled out every trick in the book to keep Kinsey's dad. As a result of the fight, the wife won. She made her husband cut off all contact with Kinsey's mom.

Kinsey's mom was so angry that she could not stand to look at the child that they created together. So she made Kinsey feel as if she was the scum of the earth. Her mother would verbally tell her how much she hated her, as her sisters constantly told her that she was so ugly. As a result, Kinsey became a loner; she began to block out everyone including her childhood friends as she wallowed in extreme anger and resentment toward her family. As her anger

Chapter 2 | Madam Oracle

began to boil over, she began to take it out on animals; she would try to kill her cat, abuse her dog and choke her hamster.

One day, her mother got so tired of looking at her; she took her and dropped her off on her father's doorstep with one bag of clothes. Kinsey cried for days—her stepmom did not care for her, and she turned her daughters against her as well. It was as if Kinsey was taken out of the pot and placed into the frying pan. Her stepmom was the meanest woman in town, who had to control everything including her husband. If Kinsey wanted to stay in the house, she had to earn her keep. She had to clean behind everyone—she cleaned windows, scrubbed floors, wash clothes, took out the garbage, etc., while her step-sisters did nothing. This child grew up associating love with cleaning up. If she wanted to get attention, she cleaned up; therefore, causing her to become a cleaning fanatic.

Kinsey never learned how to love, nor did she care about learning how. As the years clicked by, she began to hate her biological mother, sisters, step-mom, and step-sisters. Kinsey could not get over the fact that she wasn't wanted, so as she grew older, she began to hate herself more and more. It got so bad that she would unconsciously do things to make people dislike her because that became her normal. If someone appeared to take an interest in her, she would push them away. She did not feel as if she was worthy of being loved; as a result, she was not able to express it as well.

Emotional abuse has consumed this young lady's life. Today, Kinsey is still fighting with her family on both sides. She still hates them, and they hate her ways—she has gone through an extensive amount of counseling, but she refuses to let go of the past and to truly find a way to love herself. I explained to her that she was able to **Get the Information to Change Herself Out of the Bible**, but she could care less about the Bible, and she could care less about God. I would think to myself, "What a life to live without having God in it!" I was amazed at her desire to wallow.

How is it that we have our blessings at our fingertips and become so blind to its power—when all we have to do is learn how to love ourselves enough to embrace all that life has in store for us. We are so blessed and do not realize it. Every day that we wake up, we are blessed to see another day; therefore, we must not allow the past to cloud our judgment and our desire to live a fulfilled lifestyle.

Loving Oneself

The truth about love is that we all need it, we all want it, and we all deserve to have it. But the question remains, why are there so many people unsuccessful in this area? Why is it that we take our love and the love of others for granted? Why is it that we say that we love someone, but we are quick to neglect their needs, reject them, or mistreat them out of selfishness or a mere desire to control them? Of course, we all have Our Own Truth, or better yet, our own perception of what love is and what it is not. However, regardless of how much we know or do not know about love, we must get a good understanding of it, to cause love to work on our behalf.

I must also add, this is the type of love that's not sold on a shelf, it's not in a pill bottle, or better yet, the point in fact, the love that I am referring to does not have a price tag at all—IT CANNOT BE BOUGHT! Yes indeed, I will say it again—IT CANNOT BE BOUGHT! Why? It is my reasonable service to share this SECRET with the World—the answer is that it cannot be bought because it is a GIFT from within. And until we understand this fact, OUR TRUTH will always cause us to become aloof in our way of thinking, behaving, and becoming.

LOVE is free to all; and, it is especially beneficial to those who understand the Laws of Our Soulish Nature, the Laws of the Land, the Laws of the Universe, and the Laws of God regarding this free gift. Nevertheless, it may indeed cost us to apply, understand, or invest in our love for something or someone, but it is FREE with no strings attached. In my opinion, if there are strings attached—it is not free; it is conditional! It is the Conditional Love that causes us to embrace the false truths about what love is; therefore, causing us to become divided from within, divided in our relationships, and divided from our Creator, because we cannot keep our emotions in check.

Love is an underlying emotion that predicates itself on all the other positive or negative emotions that we possess. Too much love or the lack of it can cause positive or negative emotions that will strengthen or hinder our ability to balance ourselves mentally, physically, emotionally, and spiritually. Therefore, we must learn and understand the value of love, how to give it, how to receive it, how to balance it, and how to function without it. But, more importantly than anything else, here is one of my SECRETS, Love is intertwined with WISDOM! When we glean information from the mind of a truly wise person, we must take into account that this type of information is not for everyone. As a matter of fact, with the gleaning process, one must understand that they must embrace what they are gleaning, or it will slip away from them.

The truth is that WISDOM and LOVE are supreme, and it's available to everyone—Wisdom says that *"I love those who love me, and those who seek me diligently will find me"* (Proverbs 8:17). For this reason, *"The Guarded Psalms of Prayer"* helps to make understanding the Book of Proverbs easy for the elite, as well as the average person who is seeking real love and wisdom. And, one thing that I know personally is that *"wisdom is better than rubies, and all the things one may desire cannot be compared with her"* (Proverbs 8:11). I cannot place a price tag on the wisdom that God has bestowed upon me to uncover some of the Hidden Secrets of Love in the Book of Proverbs.

Although some base their love on their sexuality; nevertheless, that is only infatuation that will soon fade. Real love has zero attachments to sexuality; it has attachments to our emotions which are played out in our moral or immoral sexual acts that determine the level of wisdom or folly on our behalf. This is exactly why once

Chapter 2 | Madam Oracle

we have sex, our emotions become tied up; and God forbid if we are jumping from one sexual partner to the next—we really have emotional issues that must be reckoned with! While most would deny that they are in bondage emotionally or mentally; however, our actions, reactions, and thoughts reveal the TRUTH without us saying one word.

It is fair to say that what's not said can reveal a thousand words; especially when it comes down to the matters of the heart. I have witnessed personally how love can be used to control, manipulate, use, and abuse those who have a genuine desire to share that in which we all crave, and that is LOVE. It behooves me how love is rejected day in and day out, and the same individual who rejected the love that was freely given to them, turn around and say that no one loves them. Is this a love problem? Or, is this an emotional issue? In my opinion, it's a little bit of both. Based on the emotional rejection or perception within oneself, it is hard for them to receive the love that's offered to them at no cost. This could also veer into the mental instability status as well, especially when there has been severe psychological trauma or abuse from the past that's left unresolved or buried that has caused them to associate love with a price, hassle, fight, etc. Nevertheless, the Love of God, the Love of Self, and the Love of Others are worth more than what money can buy or any price that one would have to pay. If we can find a way to understand this one precept, we can conquer or overcome any obstacle that's trying to prevent love from coming our way or any obstacle that's trying to prevent us from giving love as well.

Often we are taught not to love ourselves, but loving who we are as a person is vital to the success of our relationships. The Bible speaks of being able to love your neighbors as you love yourself. So, that means that you are only able to love someone to the extent of how much you love yourself. I have heard some women say, "I love this man more than I love myself." I have a hard time believing that, because if you feel as if you love someone more than you love yourself—it is "INFATUATION."

Self-love is one of the keys to putting our past behind us to embrace the true greatness from within. True greatness will not show up, if we hate ourselves. We must learn how to love the good, the bad and the ugly secrets that we hold inside, while taking care of ourselves as we should. Self-love is not being conceited or selfish; it's about transforming our lives into something beautiful to benefit ourselves, and the lives of others. On the other hand, self-hatred deprives us of the opportunity to become a living testimony of love, grace, and fulfillment.

The way we love ourselves will determine how others treat us; actually, we tell others how to treat us by our attitude, actions and reactions. For example, if a man wants to be treated like a man, but his actions are childlike in nature—more than likely, he's going to be treated like a boy instead of a man. We set the tone for the way we are treated, so pay attention to the small things to ensure that the love that we have for ourselves is spread abroad to positively change lives.

When we compare ourselves with other people, we must question the love that we possess from within. Self-love allows us to accept our imperfections, understanding that God has made us unique in our very own special way. Besides, it's not a matter of being egocentric, conceited, or selfish; it's a matter of loving the skin we are in. Furthermore, if we can't love that about ourselves, it will be extremely hard to love that about someone else once the newness wears off. When it comes down to our emotions, love, and fear are the stimulating factors that will build or break down our relationships. So, falling in love with ourselves is not a bad idea, because it will make our seemingly imperfections become our small blessings. If you are having a problem loving yourself:

1. Make a list of positive affirmations and read them every day.
2. List 10 things that you like about yourself and read it every day.
3. Make your self-talk positive. If you say or think something negative about yourself, you must repeat a positive affirmation 10 times.

4. If someone says something negative about you, you respond back with something positive about yourself.

5. If someone gives you a compliment, say "thank-you."

Just remember, God broke the mold when he created us, so there is greatness in what He created. There is no need to fear it, just learn how to embrace it.

Fearfully Made

The most common emotional blocker is the fear that keeps us from truly cultivating our unique self. The surface issues that we experience from fear is by far created its own set of havoc in our lives. However, it's not too late. We have to understand the underlying root cause of why we fear whatever or whoever it is. Most often, when we are constantly hurt in relationships whether it is with a male or female, we start to build a wall of protection. The more we become hurt, the higher our walls become, and the more we close ourselves off to people, places, and things. Of course, this is our way of protecting ourselves; but, are we really protecting ourselves? The answer is no.

When we build walls or if our walls become so high, we do not allow the people, places, and things that we desire into our lives. Actually, we do not realize that we are causing our own anger, resentment, loneliness, etc. When we find ourselves dealing with walls, we will find ourselves dealing with the lack of trust. Most often, we think that having fear is a weakness, but it can be our greatest strength, if we allow ourselves the opportunity to learn through our fears, or to learn in spite of our fears. By doing so, wholeness and restoration will be waiting for us to reach out and claim the keys to freedom.

Prayer

Restore me, O' Lord—as I seek Your face and not Your hand. I pray that you bless my going out and coming in Christ Jesus, as I seek the wisdom and statues of Your Will. Father, my God which art in Heaven, open my heart, open my mind to enable me to walk in Your Divine precepts in full obedience of Your commandments, as You restore what the cankerworms have tried to devour.

The true Fisher of all men, Your word is my strength to keep me shielded from the wayward spirits that are designed to tear me down. As You catch me in the net of Your glory, I am asking that You allow the waywardness of wickedness to pass over me, to ensure that I am able to stay focused on what I need to do, as I delight in You.

My Comforter and Way Maker, You are my present help in my time of need, let me not be put to shame for walking down this path that You have set before me.

My hope rests in You to ensure that I will never thirst again in the area that I am pleading for Your restoration.

For, it is You O' Lord that I seek restoration from, it is You O' Lord that will turn my darkness into light, unveiling my vision as You did for Blind Man Bartimaeus. It is You O' Lord that can bring instant healing to my issues that have gone public—like You did for the Woman that had an issue for 12 years, and was restored immediately after pulling on the hem of Your garment.

My Lord of Hosts, it is You that can miraculously change my situation, like You did when You turned water into wine. It is You O' Lord, out of my obedience, that I will know when to drop my nets for the big catch, or when the timing is right to become a fisher of men, as You did for Simon Peter, Your disciple. It is You O' Lord that can heal my sickness and pain, as You did for the Lepers. It is You O' Lord that can multiply the provisions of my house, as You did with 2 fish and 5 loaves of bread to feed a multitude of 5000 people. It is You O' Lord that can calm the storms that are raging in my life; it is You O' Lord that can bid me to come and walk by faith and not by sight; it is You O' Lord that can bring life to the dead areas of my life; it is You, it is You, it is You. It is You O' Lord that my hope and salvation rest in. For this, O' Lord, I give thanks to You for divine restoration, while Your praises continually flow from my lips. Thank you. Amen.

Scripture Reading:

Psalms 119
Psalms 126
Psalms 143

CHAPTER 3

Guarded Genes

Throughout my journey in life, I have found that the key to living a fulfilled life is to develop a relationship with our Heavenly Father, first; then a relationship with self, and then on to building a relationship with others. If we get this out of order, chaos will soon follow in religion, in a relationship, in our ability to give/receive love, or in life period. Trust me, there is a certain order in the Universe—for example, in the morning, we will never see the sunset before the sunrise, we will never see the sunrise from the west or the sunset in the east—the day that we see that happening, we have a serious problem.

Chaos is all around us. What can we do about it? Absolutely nothing, right? Wrong. The key to overcoming the chaos is to understand it. Although, some like chaos, some do not like it, and some are conditioned to tolerate it; however, we do not have to become a victim of it. We are able to become educated in an area of our lives that has a way of keeping us paralyzed, not knowing which way to turn.

Some time ago, a few friends introduced me to this family that literally amazed me—it made my issues with my family minuscule. I could not believe this family functioned in such a way; actually, it made me appreciate my family even more. Nevertheless, I needed to find out how this family got to this state and here is what I found, *"This family was cursed back in the early 1900's. William and Jallee got married at a very young age; although they were both immature, it did not stop them from having a family. Every year it seemed as if Jallee was pushing out a baby, in total she had 9 girls and 4 boys. William loved having a big family, but there was one problem—he was broke, and he had very little money to support them. Even though they ate the leftovers from the restaurant where he worked, it wasn't enough. He had to do something.*

One day, William had this bright idea; he could make more than enough money with his 9 daughters. So, he began to prostitute his daughters for money, food, water and moonshine; and used his sons to sell what they had left over. Jallee pleaded with him to stop prostituting his children, but he was adamant about not going to bed hungry ever again. Yes, William was a cook by day and a true hustler by night—living a well-to-do life.

His daughters grew up to hate him. As they began to have babies, he would sell them too. William became ruthless; he would sell anything he could get his hands on, except for his wife. He knew that his wife held all of his secrets, and he knew that he needed her to cook, clean and take care of his kids—so he dared not to cross her. However, she did not know about the family that he kept across town. All the years that she allowed him to prostitute her children, he kept another wife across town with 2 daughters in private school. Once Jallee found out about his prestigious outside family—there was never a peaceful moment in the house until the day she died. Some believed that she died from a broken heart, and some believed that she could no longer live with her conscience; but one thing they do know, is that chaos ruled the family from that day forward.

As the children grew older, they would fight each other like they were enemies. They were ruthless like their father; they did not respect each other, and they could care less about respecting other people; but, Leslie, in particular, was the spitting image of her father. She was indeed a hustler by trade and a prostitute every now and then; however, she refused to prostitute her children. She knew that she could make more than enough money selling moonshine and running numbers. Living the fast life of drinking, smoking, and having fun with men, she was hell on wheels. This woman had a mouth on her; she cursed like a sailor and would do almost anything for money. Her kids began to follow in her footsteps—they would do anything for money as well. This one day she scored really big with running her numbers, her oldest daughter Lily asked her for a loan. She then cursed her daughter out and said, "You have a money-maker between your legs, go use it and stop asking me for money!" Her daughter was appalled, but she took her mom's advice.

Lily began to follow in her mom's footsteps—doing anything to make money. She became so jealous of her mom that she had *someone to rob her. This was the ultimate betrayal for her mom, and when she realized who was robbing her—she fought back. The guy could not risk getting caught or exposing Lily, so he shot her—killing her instantly.*

Of course, Lily has to live with that dreadful memory for the rest of her life as betrayal continues through her bloodline. Now, Lily has turned to legally suing people with fictitious claims extorting over $500,000.00 in claims thus far. Her children are following in her footsteps as well suing, robbing, and undercover prostitution. This family will do anything for money, and they do not feel as if they have ever done anything wrong.

Lily has this one daughter in particular; she is the greatest con artist ever. She knows how to cheat you out of a dime when you only have a nickel—she's just that good. Actually, she picked up where her mother and grandmother left off—she was determined to do what she needed to do to survive.

A history of sexual, mental, and emotional abuse has plagued this family beyond what we could ever imagine. As a result of this genetic chaos, this plague has not stopped as of yet; it's already into its 5th generation. The last update that I have of this family is that William died a year after Leslie was killed. Lily is waiting to cash in on the insurance policies that she has on her children as well as her grandchildren; while living off the money on her last lawsuit of $200,000.00. This family is still permeated with prostitution, identity theft, bribery, robbery, and suing on a more sophisticated level. The power of manipulation has clouded this family's way of thinking, and I believe that they really enjoy the chaos. If they really wanted to change, they could—if they would just put their past behind them, exercise the power of forgiveness, fast and pray—it would break this generational curse. I really wonder how long this family will continue in their folly; however, I could not help but to reflect back on Luke 6:44. It says, *"For every tree is known by its own fruit. For men do not gather figs from thorns, nor do they gather grapes from a bramble bush."*

Change comes when we make the necessary sacrifices to put dead or chaotic things behind us. What's in the past is in the past! There is no need to bury ourselves in the things of old. Actually, it is the things of old that keep our heads buried in the sand of mental anguish. Furthermore, when we allow ourselves to become too mentally entangled in someone or something, rest assured that emotional bondage will soon follow like a thief in the night. Yes, most often it will take more than we are willing to give. Our willingness to put away dead things gives us the power to cope, the power to forgive, and the power to eliminate our sensitivities of being misunderstood. Every day in conjunction with the use of *"The Guarded Psalms of Prayer"* provides us with an opportunity to live better than we did the day before. Furthermore, when we allow ourselves to live in victory, we then open the door to succeed in places that we never knew existed.

Putting things behind you will definitely give you a boost of confidence to move forward, when others are looking at the impossibilities at hand. God can and will do exceedingly and abundantly above all that you can ask or think as long as you trust, forgive, and believe that He can and will.

Prayer

Father, my God, in the Name of Jesus, my soul pants for You. You are a breath of living water that quenches the thirst from within with the power of forgiveness. Therefore, I hereby forgive anyone who has trespassed against me, deceived me, angered me, provoked me, hurt me, upset me, offended me, used me, or sinned against me in any way, shape, or form. However, before I go any further in this healing process, I first and foremost, forgive myself. Therefore, I am justified in invoking the Spirit of Forgiveness to permeate into the depths of my soul, releasing me from anything that would cause me to hoard secret acts of revenge or retaliation.

As the Spirit of Forgiveness is upon me, My God, allow the words of my mouth and the meditations of my heart to become holy and acceptable in Your sight, as I embark upon this journey. Father, please allow me to be forgiven by others for any known or unknown, accidental or willful, intentional or unintentional sinful actions, whether by word, deed, thoughts, creed, or attitude. If I have brought about any ungodly action or reaction that's outside of Your will, let me change in ways that make it easy for me to avoid paths of hurtfulness to others.

As forgiveness takes place from within me, Lord allow me to change my ways to ensure that Your divine grace and mercy radiates through my actions, reactions, and attitude. Therefore, I am able to pick up Your Divine Favor; and, regardless of what others think about the power of my ability to forgive, I know that beyond a shadow of a doubt that You are guiding my every footstep. Besides, to be guided by Your presence, means that unforgiveness cannot take up residence where You reside.

My Merciful Redeemer, my hope rests in You; adorn me with an inner peace that surpasses all human understanding. For this O' Lord, I give thanks to You, as Your praises will be continually on my lips. Amen.

<u>Scripture Reading:</u>

Psalms 25
Psalms 105

CHAPTER 4

Guarded Insanity

Life has a way of rubbing us the wrong way, especially when we want something or someone really bad. I realized this when a bunch of my friends came over to my house for a Pillow Talk session. As we began to tell wild stories about ourselves, this new attendee, Macy had the most unusual story about "The Mask of Insanity." *Her mask of insanity began at an early age of 16 when she ran off with her childhood sweetheart. He pretended to love her, and she gave in to charm; not realizing that she would become pregnant. That's where she put on her 1st mask; she hid her pregnancy up until her 7th month. By that time, it was too late for an abortion. Her mom was furious, and she was not willing to take care of another child. Macy had to make a decision—she decided to keep her child hoping that the father would stay with her. After telling her mom about the decision, her mom put her out of her house. She called her boyfriend to tell him what happened, and he yelled at her saying, "That's not my child." Macy wandered the streets for a few days, and finally ended up in a shelter until she had the baby. She felt so alone, with no place to go until she met this young man who promised her the world on one condition. He wasn't going to take care of another man's child, and she agreed that he should not have to.*

A few days later, Macy took her newborn baby boy to his grandparent's house to visit, and she never went back for him. She had to wear that mask of disgrace of leaving her child to be with another man. Eventually, she got over it as she became pregnant from her new man, as they lived in their own little façade of temporary happiness. After her newness had worn off, she realized that he was an abuser, alcoholic, and drug addict. While pregnant, he began to beat her for everything, even for looking at him the wrong way. She lived under an enormous amount of guilt, pressure, and resentment. Macy sat at home all day thinking about how she gave up her son for this man, only to receive beatings in return. The more she thought about it, the angrier she became.

This one rainy day, her boyfriend came in really toasted, stumbling all over the house looking for his cigarettes that he had bought 2 days ago. He knew that they were in the house somewhere, so he asked Macy to help look for them, and she refused. She did not feel like searching around the house for his smokes. He became furious with her, knocking her out of the chair, as she stood up, he began to beat her like there was no tomorrow. Macy thought he was going to kill her, so she grabbed a lamp, hit him with it and ran out of the house.

Chapter 4 | Madam Oracle

She ran to a friend's house hoping that she didn't kill him: however, after receiving a few stitches, her boyfriend came looking for her, begging for her to come back home—and she did. Things went okay for a couple of weeks, but his drug habits became worse—he began to shoot-up.

While pregnant, Macy met Rick. He was a pretty decent guy, who worked hard and made a pretty good salary. She had a fear of living on the streets again, and she was willing to do anything not to go back. After seeing Rick for a few months, she felt as if she had hit the jackpot. However, she had to figure out a way to break away from her boyfriend, because she knew that he was not going to give up easily. So she waited for the opportune moment—she knew that he liked shooting up, so she put water in his needle. When he shot up that night, it stopped his heart. She called the paramedics; they got him back to breathing again; however, he did suffer damage to the brain, which left him in a wheelchair for the rest of his life. There wasn't an investigation because he had a history of drug use and an extensive criminal history—they felt as if he was no longer a threat to society and he was better off in a wheelchair.

Macy got what she wanted, but she had to put on the 2nd mask. She could never let anyone know what she did; especially Rick, her new victim. Of course, Rick wasn't a saint, but he had money, and he was willing to take care of Macy. This was her ticket to freedom, and she was not going to allow anyone to take it away from her. After having the child with her previous boyfriend, she immediately became pregnant with Rick's child. He was so excited—he was like a kid in a candy store. After she had locked Rick down, they got married. She had her mask on for a few years *until the lust of her flesh got the best of her. She did not love Rick as a wife should, and for some odd reason, Rick knew it. However, he had a family; she got what she wanted, he got what he wanted, and there was no reason to rock the boat, right? Wrong. Macy got buck-wild. She had a thing for men in uniforms; therefore, falling head-over-heels in love with this married police officer. Cory, the police officer, was only looking for a fling while Macy was looking for a new man. Cory played Macy like a little fiddle, as she was blinded by her own lust of greed.*

After carrying on with the relationship for years, Cory asked Macy to set-up one of her friends from high school in an undercover drug bust. In the name of love, she agreed. She went undercover, sparking a sexual relationship with this guy; while getting all of this guy's personal information. She wore a wire, took pictures, etc.—she went all out to set-up her friend. Why was she doing all of this? All of this was done for the love of Cory. Eventually, her friend got busted, went to prison and Cory dumped her. She was devastated; she cried for months. Now to add insult to injury, the friend that she set up was killed in prison. What a life to live, right? Wrong. She became vindictive, so she put on her 3rd mask.

Macy is a married woman, and her husband did not have a clue about the type of woman he was dealing with. However, she was not going to stop until she made Cory feel the hurt and embarrassment that she had to endure. One day, she came up with a plan; she sparked a relationship with his best friend, who was also married. Somehow, she got him on her good side to arrange a ménage à trois with him and another police officer. After the event, they talked about her so bad. Cory was so humiliated by her acts that he could not stand to ever look at her ever again.

Chapter 4 | Madam Oracle

Macy was on the prowl again, looking for her next victim, while Rick took the time to raise the children. It's sad to say, but being a mother was not her highest priority; she wanted to experience the fairytale romance of catching her Mr. Right. After searching for years, ignoring her family, she found him. Actually, she met her match. It was love at first sight—she was looking for love, and he was looking for a victim. He told her everything that she wanted to hear—he spoiled her with fancy gifts, he took her to fancy restaurants, and he painted a picture of love that she had always dreamt about. He became her world as she lost interest in her husband, her kids, and motherly responsibilities.

He finally convinced her to move out—she packed her bags to move in with Mr. Right, while leaving her kids with Rick. She planned on divorcing Rick and marrying Mr. Right and living the fairytale dream. She did not realize that she had been planting seeds from the ripe old age of 16, and her seeds were getting ready to break ground.

As she lived the single life for about 6 months, her children became more devastated than ever—they realized that she was not coming back. They could not believe that their mother left them behind for another man. Of course, Rick was angry, but he still wanted his wife back. He and the children begged her to come back, but she said, "She needed to live her life." She filed for divorce, in hopes to marry Mr. Right.

After the divorce was final, she asked Mr. Right, "When are we getting married?" He said, "Never." She asked, "Why?" He said, "You want me to marry you, so you can leave me like you left your husband and children!" She was stunned. She left her husband for an empty promise—she burned the bridges with her now ex-husband and her children. How could she possibly go back? How could Mr. Right become Mr. Wrong?

Mr. Wrong had her right where he wanted her—desperate. He knew that once she became desperate, she would do anything for him. And, he was right! He began to brainwash her into thinking that he was the only person in the world that loved her. He cut her off from her family and friends while he began to do a good job on her mentally—as her conscious began to work on the other side.

Macy was an emotional wreck! She felt as if God was punishing her for her past, but she could not find a way to ask God to forgive her. As she wallowed, she became more desperate— Mr. Wrong's goal was to turn Macy into a high-class call girl. And, it was working. If she did not do it, he would beat her. This lifestyle was so embarrassing for her; she would not tell a soul. The more she did it, the easier it became for her until he brainwashed her into getting her oldest daughter back. She did not want her daughter to know that she was a high-class call girl, so she allowed her daughter to stay with him. Her daughter did not want to stay with Mr. Wrong, because she knew what was going to happen—she could see the lust in his eyes. As Macy began to leave, her daughter ran behind her saying, "Mommy, please do not leave me, please mommy do not leave me." And she left anyway. Against her better judgment, she put her daughter in a situation to be molested by her so-called boyfriend.

All for the Sake of Love....after all of the physical, mental, and emotional abuse given and received by Macy, she still refuses to fast, pray, and ask for forgiveness; as a result, she continues on a downward spiral that hasn't stopped yet.

Just to have Mr. Wrong in her life, she sacrificed her daughter's future—she knew how he was and what he was capable of doing, but she did not care. She only thought about herself, and to her, nothing else mattered. After suffering many health problems, Mr. Wrong finally let her go because her money-maker stopped making money. Macy is still reaping the harvest of the seeds that she has sown over the years, and wish that she could have a second chance at making her family work. She is alone living her past over and over again as the fruits of her labor continued to fall at her feet that drove her mentally insane. Rick and his daughters are living a great life by embracing the power of prayer, and the hidden treasures of using *"The Guarded Psalms of Prayer;"* therefore, releasing them from becoming victims of Macy's past mistakes.

Where there's a longing, we must take into account the seeds that we have planted over the years. When we take into account what we are giving, then we are better able to understand what we are receiving. My friend, everything, and I mean everything we do, say, and think becomes a SEED! It is up to us to determine whether or not our seeds will become positively or negatively planted, discarded, or held on to.

Life has a way of granting us the conditions in which we subconsciously choose. When given a little time, the seed that we plant can and will produce after its own kind, regardless of when, what, how, where and why it's planted. But, what about the seeds that remain unplanted? Great question, "NO HARVEST!" There are some seeds that we need to plant, and there are some that we should not plant.

Your lifeline is in the seeds that you are planting. From me to you, do not think for a minute that you are able to supersede the laws of the land, "SEED, TIME, and HARVEST." What you plant, in time, you will receive; however, you are able to uproot and discard seeds planted through your attitude, actions, and reactions, in conjunction with the use of *"The Guarded Psalms of Prayer"."* Today, choose your seeds carefully, as you discard the negative seeds that are intentionally or unintentionally planted by others.

Prayer

Defend me, defend me, defend me, my God which art in Heaven. I am crying out to You to defend me, my family, my mind, my soul, my body, my spirit, my life, and most of all, my salvation in the mighty Name of Jesus. You are indeed my help in my time of need, please do not remain silent or turn a deaf ear to my innocent cry for help, because it is through You my help cometh. It is through You that my weaknesses become strengths, it is through You that my fears become confidence, and My God, it is through You that my tears become laughter. Thereupon, I humbly come before You, pleading that You do not allow me to fall by the wayside with the woes of the evil doers, or the woes from within the depths of my very own soul.

Father, by divine decree, let no unjust actions from the wicked affect me, or my well-being in any way, shape or form, as You strengthen me to go forth in Your will. Lord, for the dark areas of my life, I pray that You bring light to those areas as Your grace and mercy become illuminated through me. For You are indeed the rock of my salvation, whom shall I fear—I know that we all appear right in our own eyes; but Lord, clear my vision, clear my heart, and clear my mind of all unrighteousness that I may have knowingly or unknowingly caused. And, for that reason, I seek forgiveness in those areas, in the mighty Name of Jesus, as I set the record straight on the secret issues of my heart that will keep me defeated if I do not rectify them right now.

More upon this Lord, You know the intents of my heart, and it is You who prevents my feet from slipping and falling; therefore, I declare and decree, according to Your Word that no weapon formed against me shall prosper. Henceforth, there is one thing that I know, the weapons of warfare are not carnal, but for the pulling down of strongholds in Christ Jesus. For that reason, with clean hands and a pure heart, I lift Your name on high as I give this battle over to You, so that the strongholds that I am dealing with can create an element of victory on Your behalf, as well as mine. And for this,

O' Lord, I give thanks to You, while Your praises continually flow from my lips. Thank you. Amen.

Scripture Reading:

Psalms 11
Psalms 23
Psalms 28
Psalms 44

CHAPTER 5

Guarded Time

As *"The Guarded Psalms of Prayer"* has its way in our lives, it will tell us everything we need to know if we just listen to it. However, I advise everyone that has an ear to hear, to be cautious about developing a deaf ear to reality, and to the wealth of wisdom left behind before it's too late. However, I am so glad that it wasn't too late for Steve.

Steve was considered to be an all-time playboy; he had women for every day of the week. Actually, he enjoyed ignoring women to drive them crazy. This is one of the rules men use to drive women to chase them. He was out one night, this one young lady that fell victim to his games said to him, "You need God in your life." He said to her, "I am God." This young lady could not believe that he was so arrogant. As she walked away, she said, "One day you will see how much of a God you are!" He blew her off and continued to mingle with the pretty girls in the club.

For some reason, it seemed as if Steve hated God, and if you spoke about God to him, he had a great debate for you. Oddly enough, he actually made it his business to discredit God, and what you believe in. He was ruthless when it came down to being a Christian. If you proclaimed to be Christian abstaining from sex, he would make it his business to break you. Actually, he loved the women in the church—he said that they are the easiest to break because they are desperate; and, the only reason that they go to church is to find a man that could pay their bills. So, he sold them a dream of paying their bills; they gave him what he wanted, and he kicks them to the curb. He had women crying, fighting, and depressed over him. Can you imagine giving up your goodies to a man, just so he could prove that God is not your source of strength?

The truth about Steve is that he treated women the way his mother was treated by a certain man that proclaimed to love her. As soon as that God fearing man impregnated Steve's mom with him, he left her without any explanation; therefore, causing Steve to grow up angry, hating his father. Actually, Steve's father was a pulpit player who manipulated every woman in the church, including his mother. As a result, Steve's mom had to wear the burden of shame during his whole childhood—although, she became a well-educated woman, she never married any other man, because she could not get over the pain. Steve had to watch his mother go through the pain of rejection and loneliness; therefore, he made a secret promise to himself that he was going to make every woman feel that pain that his mother had to endure. As an adult, he kept his promise to himself, but it came with some serious consequences that he ignored on a daily basis.

Even though Steve had a lot of women, he was still lonely. He could not understand how he could have his choice of women, men on occasion, and still not be fulfilled. So instead, he began to drink and party a little more—it did not work. He tried hanging out with his professional friends—it did not work. Nothing seemed to satisfy the longing from within Steve's soul. It was so sad that behind that façade of being Mr. Fabulous Playboy, he was a lonely boy in need of spiritual healing. The more he played women, the bigger the longing became within his soul. The more he secretly dabbled with men on occasion, the longing then became pits of pure shame and total regret.

He went to see his mother one day, and this old lady called him over to tell him something. He started not to go, but it would have been rude of him not to—so he went. The lady appeared to be a little strange as she began to reach out to hold his hand. She said, "Baby, God is watching your every move. He has a calling on your life, and you will never find happiness outside of his calling. The more you run, the bigger the hole will become in your heart." Steve pulled away rather quickly while this little nudge pulled at his heart.

He felt as if he could not turn away from the life, the girls, the money, the fame, the friends, and the power. He had a sincere problem with appearing weak; he was willing to respect God, but he was not willing to become weak for Him. As he left his mom's house, Steve had an accident that left him clinging to life. He knew deep within his heart that this accident wasn't about him; it was about God's purpose.

As he laid there for months, he was God alright—very few people came to visit him. The friends that he thought he had never came. The girls that enjoyed spending time with him never came. The money, power, and lifestyle that he had were meaningless at this point. Steve had plenty of time to think about what he could not let go of, and what he now had to embrace. He had to make a decision to walk in purpose or die not living his purpose—so he made a choice 3 months after the accident happened.

I personally, could not believe that it took Steve that long to decide to do the will of God. However, Steve has totally recovered from his accident, and he has found that *"The Guarded Psalms of Prayer"* really works. As a result of learning how to fast and pray, there is no turning back for him. Steve is now a well-known minister, married, and has 2 children—his life has changed in ways that he could only have dreamt about. As a matter of fact, He has saved more souls than you would care to imagine; and now, I see why God had to get rid of Steve's distractions.

When we are distracted, it will cause the best of us to jump over treasure to pick up junk. As a matter of fact, distractions have a way of distorting the value of the people, places, and things that we have passed up to fill a temporary void. But, make no mistake about it, when it's all said and done, the value of the dollar can purchase a lot of things, but character is not one of them. When we become caught up in the issues of life, we tend to let our guards down in the hope of receiving attention to fill an unrecognizable void. When we fill that void with something other than what we are really missing, we will find ourselves trying to undo things that are already done, doing things that we should have left alone from the beginning, or attracting people, places, and things that are out of character for us. Furthermore, it's highly impossible to receive or attract the treasures of life if we have too much junk blocking our way.

Most often, your treasure is right under your nose! However, it's up to you whether or not you take the time or the opportunity to get rid of the junk and sift through the dirt to get to what rightfully belongs to you. From me to you, your overlooked treasures will always keep their hidden value whether it's visible to you or not.

Prayer

Father, my God in the Name of Jesus, I am seeking Your face on how to develop trust for myself, with others, and with You. Lord, You know the hurts, pains, and betrayals that I have endured in the past that has contributed to my troubled heart. For it is Your power that will bring salvation to my distrustful weariness; therefore, I give this issue to You, I am praying for healing in those areas, as well as healing regarding my environmental conditioning of my thoughts, actions, and beliefs that have contributed to my situation.

Father, as I learn how to trust my instincts, as well as those small nudges from within, help me to lean not to my own understanding regarding the ways in which You are going to bless me or direct me. For I know that Your ways are not mine, and my ways are not Yours—so I pray that You remove the fear and doubt from within me that would cause me to second-guess Your will or Your way.

My God, I know that Your presence is real in my life, I know that without You there would not be me, I know that I am a product of my own human nature, I also know that there is a time and place for everything under the sun. For this reason, I count myself not to be apprehended, because as long as the sun rises in the east and sets in the west every day, as long as there is morning and evening every day, and as long as time does not stop, I know that Your divine order is in place, giving me hope for tomorrow. And, according to Your word regarding trust, if I ask for it, believe that I have it, and it will be mine—so I lay claim to it right now, in the Name of Jesus as I overflow with the trustworthy power of the Holy Spirit.

As I exude confidence and peace in my life, I don't want to just say I trust You, I desire for my life, my actions, my reactions, my thoughts, my beliefs, and conversations to become a representation of my trust in You. Thus, giving me the ability to be a living testimony to speak life into the people, places, and things that need what You have to offer. And for this, O' Lord, I give thanks to You, while Your praises continually flow from my lips. Amen.

<u>**Scripture Reading:**</u>

Psalms 14
Psalms 30
Psalms 45
Psalms 46
Psalms 67
Psalms 135
Psalms 138

CHAPTER 6

The Guarded Psalms of Prayer!

In order to embrace *"The Guarded Psalms of Prayer,"* we need to pay attention to what's going on from within us, as well as around us. Our path of mastery is determined by our ability to reach beyond our self-imposed limitations to assume responsibility for our actions, reactions, and the lack thereof.

"The Guarded Psalms of Prayer" says that it is easier to blame someone else for our problems, but guess what? It doesn't solve anything. If we take a moment to look back over our lives, we will find that the issues that we are having right now, are the issues that we did not pray about, the issues that we did not seek God about, or the issues that we did not exercise the wisdom that was available to us at that time. Therefore, shifting the blame has become easier, or better yet, emotionally comforting than to take responsibility for our actions, reactions, or the lack thereof.

The best example that I can give regarding *"The Guarded Psalms of Prayer"* is to tell Mason's story about an extreme bout with spiritual abuse. Actually, when Mason began to tell me her story, I was in great disbelief, until she showed evidence validating her ordeal.

As life would have it, Mason grew up as a sheltered child, who did not realize that her weaknesses would expose her to the real world. Nevertheless, Mason knew what type of man that she wanted, and did not care about voicing her opinion about her likes and dislikes. As destiny would have it, this one particular guy named Eddie, took a special liking to Mason; although she was very cordial, she made it known that she wasn't interested by a small gesture of turning up her nose. Well, Eddie was offended by this gesture, which made him determined to make Mason his woman of choice.

Oddly enough, Mason began to take a liking to Eddie after many encounters with him. She thought that it was strange that she was taking a liking to him, but she blew it off thinking that God was teaching her a lesson about being too picky. As the relationship progressed, her soul was saying that he wasn't the one, but her mind justified her strange behavior. She began to go against everything she believed in—she stopped praying, she stopped reading the Bible; she stopped meditating; she basically stopped everything that kept her spiritually rooted and grounded. Although, Mason questioned her actions, she quickly justified them as taking a break from God. As Mason began to fall from grace, she would ask herself constantly, how can a person take a break from God? If the truth is told, she knew that she was taking a downward spiral with this man; but, for some odd reason, she could not help herself or did not want to.

After months of puppy love, the infatuation began to wear off, while reality began to set in. Let Mason tell it; the relationship got boring; Eddie was out of her league, and he knew it—He felt that he had to keep her spiritually grounded in something, or she would pull away from him. So, he invited her to an event that he was hosting, and when they got there, Mason felt out of place. The people at the event began dancing, spinning around, blowing fire, chanting, etc.; she had no idea that she was dating a Houngan (Voodoo Priest). Once she realized who he was, she ran out of the building—she got angry with God, because she felt that He let her down. After the event, she was so afraid of him and his practices; but, for some odd reason, she stayed with him. Although she felt stupid for staying, but she had no desire to leave him. Mason made it clear that she would not partake in his religious practices; however, that did not stop him from trying to draw her in. After many years of standing her ground on his religious practices, he finally gave up on trying to draw her in, but for some reason, she could not find her way back into the arms of God. She just could not make that connection, until her mom changed the rules to the game.

Mason was still a little naïve; she did not even realize that her mom had a crush on her Houngan boyfriend. Furthermore, she did not know that her mom and boyfriend were secretly having an affair behind her back. This arrogant good for nothing man, began to date the mother, in order to keep the daughter bound spiritually, because he knew that Mason's greatest weakness was her mother. Every time Mason began to pull away from Eddie, her mom would do something to emotionally traumatize her, and then she would go running back to him for comfort. Like clockwork, Eddie would be waiting for her with open arms to draw her back in again, as she could not see the trees for the forest—she just wanted someone to give her what she could never get from her mother, which was love. She often wondered how the lack of love from her mother could keep her with a man that she was not in love with; but, she blew it off, not realizing that she was spiritually blind to reality due to her weakness for love.

Even though Mason was going through something with Eddie, she never lost hope. She knew that if she did not give up on God, He would not give up on her—she knew within the depths of her soul that He would bring her out of that situation one day. Finally, the scales were removed from her eyes when she and Eddie were engaged in a fun-loving conversation; then all of a sudden, her mom calls Eddie's cell phone. Eddie did not tell her that it was her mom calling; however, she knew her mom's voice. As he indulged in the conversation, Mason could hear her mom confiding in Eddie, revealing personal information that should not be discussed with her boyfriend. As Mason listens to the ultimate betrayal, her mom made a powerhouse statement that opened her eyes—she said, "My daughter hates me, because she thinks that I am in love with you." Mason dropped her head, and began to cry—she knew at that moment her mom wanted Eddie for herself, and that something was not right about their relationship. Eddie cut the conversation short with her mom, as Mason fell apart emotionally before his very eyes—riddled with pain, she cried all night long. She knew that her mom was treacherous when it came down to a man—as a child, she saw her mom cheat with her best friend's husband, she saw her mom cheat with her dad's close friends, and she saw her mom cheat with co-workers; but, she never thought that her mom would cheat with her child's boyfriend. Wow, what would provoke a woman to cheat with her own child's man? Is it money? Is it sex? Is it envy? Is it greed? Is it control? Or, is it just being trifling? Who knows, but her conscience will soon become her guide!

As time went on, Mason began to watch and pray about her situation while drifting away from Eddie emotionally. Then she began to drift away mentally; and once she escaped the mental enslavement, she was able to see how Eddie controlled her, she was able to see how he was cheating on her, she was able to see how he was using her, she was able to see how he manipulated her, she was able to see how he tried to keep her from reading the Bible, and she was able to see how he became her mom's personal maintenance man right under her nose. However, this was only the beginning of Mason's torture—Eddie, her boyfriend, the Spiritualist, realized that he was losing his grip on her. The more he began to perform rituals to control her, the more she prayed for God to release her. This woman was indeed in a spiritual battle—now, this is what I would call sleeping with the enemy. Mason, had some real issues at this point; but, she was willing to fight for her freedom, because Eddie crossed the line when he started fooling around with her mother.

As fate would have it, I ran into Mason at a church gathering, she explained her situation to me, and asked me to pray with her about her situation. In the middle of our prayer, Mason began to vomit to no avail—I explained to her that God was trying to purge her from the situation she was in. I also told her that she needed to *stop having sex with that man, if she wanted to break free. Once God gets her out of this situation, she must never look back—no matter what happens, she must stand her ground. I gave her a prayer to read every day, and I explained to her how to use the Power of Psalms to help her with her spiritual battle.*

As a few months rolled by, she had to live with Eddie mocking her about how weak her God is. He also stated that she needed something stronger than the Bible to shake him off. Nevertheless, Mason kept praying and reading her Bible, then all of a sudden, out of nowhere, her life began to change for the better. She moves out, eager to move on with her life, and here comes Eddie, trying to rope her back in again. She was tempted; but, she remembered our conversation about not looking back. The more she pulled away from Eddie, the more desperate he became—he began to pull out little tricks to shake her emotionally, but it did not work. He tried little stunts to shake her mentally; it did not work. He started damaging her property; it did not work. He tried to sift her spiritually; it did not work. He was at a loss; he finally realized that God is indeed more powerful than he was.

So, he decided to let go of Mason; however, in doing so, he needed someone to blame—so he decided to make Mason's mom pay for what she caused with that one inappropriate, untimely phone call. When they say Karma is no joke, they mean it—low and behold, Eddie decided to drive Mason's mom crazy with one of his rituals as compensation for the pain that he has to endure for losing the one woman that he truly loved.

Mason learned the power of prayer, in conjunction with reading applicable scriptures from the Book of Psalms;

as a result, she finally has peace in her life. Her faith in God is unshakeable after that ordeal with Eddie; and, she is now married to a wonderful man who really loves her. Eddie is still running from woman to woman, looking for Mason inside of each one of them. Mason's mom is still mentally unstable, and refuses to admit to any of her wrongdoings.

The Book of Psalms is powerful, and it works! I have found that in order to open up the floodgates of our *"Mental Mastery,"* we must learn how to effectively pray for it. When we learn how to use the Book of Psalms in conjunction with our daily prayers, it invokes the Power of the Holy Spirit to release the Wisdom of our past, present, and future. For everyone will have this cycle that will incorporate seed, time, and harvest; sunrise, and sunset; morning, afternoon, and evening; spring, summer, fall, and winter; and so on. However, in the midst of the cycles of Mother Nature, we have the cycles of life; and, this is where our *"Mental Mastery"* is designed to make all things work together for our good if we believe in the power that is hidden within the Book of Psalms.

Our daily walk is indeed a journey, and it is through this journey that we determine our end result. Of course, I believe in destiny, but our destiny is depending upon the choices that we make or the lack thereof. Therefore, if we have a desire to overcome, rebound, and triumph over the trials that we are destined to have—that would indeed make our lives a stream of peace that is unknown to the natural man, unless this Wisdom of the Holy Spirit is involved. This powerful tool helps us to lean not to our own understanding; therefore, developing a faith that will allow blessings to follow us, along with a supernatural covering that will put our enemies at bay.

The Book of Psalms allows us to take biblical prayers and make them our own based on the situation, circumstance, or event that's present in our lives. It also helps us to get on one accord with God, especially when we do not know what to pray for, or how to pray. I have found that some people use the Psalms only when needed; but, in order to receive the best results, we should recite a Psalm every day, especially for giving thanks, or to exercise gratefulness. We do not need a degree to have an effective prayer; all we need is the right tools to enable favor and grace to fall upon our prayers. I have found in my Walk with God that using proper protocol, proper technique, along with a little eloquence goes a long way. I am not saying go overboard when praying; I am saying exercise some Biblical Principles, humility, and reverence when praying—God will open up the windows of Heaven, where we will not have room enough to store our blessings, GUARANTEED!

Prayer
Father my God, in the Name of Jesus, today I break the ties that bind me; and, with the Blood of the Lamb, I cut

every cord that's trying to knowingly or unknowingly control me. I decree and declare that all soul-ties created in my name be untied right now, as I renounce all ill-will or the violation of my free will that has caused me to become a puppet on a string. I command my Warring Angels to destroy anything that's not conducive to my well-being or the will that You have set for my life. From this point on, no ground can hold the ties that bind my soul without my permission, in the Name of Jesus. As I speak it into the atmosphere, it is so.

I bind Satan, along with the works of the enemy; therefore, I will no longer be under a powerful spirit of control or anyone who is trying to manipulate me with the spirit of ungodliness. The spirit of loneliness and confusion has no place in my life, so I cast it into the pits of hell from whence it came. My mind is clear, my mind is one with Christ Jesus; for on this day, I decree and declare that the soul ties between (person's name) and I, be broken in the Name of Jesus. I break it and I release him/her; therefore I am free to become the person that I have been destined to be and meet the people of my true destiny.

In the Name of Jesus, I come against, bind, and cast down into the pits of Hell every messenger spirit or kindred spirit that's revealing private information about me—I break down the lines of communication. From this day forward, my life will be covered by the Blood of Jesus, and the supply of my personal information is now cut off. Seeing into my past, present, and future is the thing of the past, without my consent, I block all access to the secrets of my heart.

My eyes are open, I am now able to detect the tricks of the enemy—I take authority over what God has blessed me with. Whatever I have lost, I did not need it for the purpose that God has for me. I firmly believe that anything that truly belongs to me, God will protect it; therefore, I loose myself immediately, completely, permanently, and continually from the negative, unholy ties that bind my soul, in the Name of Jesus.

My Strength and Redeemer, as You heal the pain, I ask that You completely restore me—so that I will never thirst again, as You place Your Wings of protection around me to protect me from the wiles of the enemy. Lord, I am standing on Your word that no weapon formed against me shall prosper, they will send it out— but it will go down, in the Name of Jesus. I declare that all evil intents will be stopped directly in its track as I embrace the fullness of life.

Father, Your Word will not return to me void or empty, as I trust and believe that You will perform Your Word according to scripture. Therefore, I cancel out any form of revenge, retaliation, or getting even from the realm of the spirit against me, my family, my possessions, or my job in any way, shape, or form. I also know that beyond a shadow of a doubt, if I am at peace with You, You will be at peace with me as I am richly rewarded and surrounded with the shield of favor on high while my enemies become my footstool.

Chapter 6 | Madam Oracle

Henceforth, I am covered by the Blood of the Lamb, so I decree and declare that anything that is not of You, O'Lord—pass over me, my family, and anyone that I hold dear to my heart. In the Name of Jesus. Thank you. Amen.

Scripture Reading:

Psalms 31
Psalms 36
Psalms 91

CHAPTER 7

Get Out of Your Own Way!

Perception, perception, perception—we can't get away from it. When we walk, our perception is there. When we talk, our perception is there. When we think, our perception is there. When we take action, our perception is there. No matter what we do, our perception has a way of tracking us down. Actually, my best example is this con artist Tiffany. *She was a little capricious, but she has a way with people—she could get any type of information that she wanted by playing dumb. She often cracked jokes about prying into the lives of others; actually, getting the dirt on people was her favorite pastime.*

Prying and snooping was her thing, and she knew it. Tiffany would steal the identity of someone right under their nose. She started with her family members, and then graduating to anyone she could benefit from. As she lived up to her reputation, she was not to be trusted with anything or anyone. Although Tiffany pretended to be an airhead, she kept a file on everyone. If she knew their name, she had a file on them—she documented everything, including her sexual partners, and their type of activities. Tiffany believed that everyone had something to hide, and it's her God-given duty to uncover it, while doing her best to keep her own life private.

As I got to know Tiffany a little better, I realized that Tiffany had some skeletons that she needed to keep hidden. This lady had secrets that would put her and others under the jailhouse. As a child, she began seducing her uncle for lunch money, and enough money to buy her friends as well. The more she did it, the easier it became and the more she enjoyed it. She continued that for years until she got bored, needing more than just lunch money. As a result, she decided to step up her game; however, her game plan was not a plan of a normal child. I could not believe that after she had blackmailed her uncle enough, she decided to seduce her mom and her sister's boyfriends for money. She felt as if her mom and sister were too fat and ugly to please their man, so she decided to please them for money, and a ticket out of the ghetto. Did it work? Absolutely. Tiffany moved on with her life and her secrets—she no longer had to live in a roach-infested house, nor did she have to deal with the guilt of what she was doing, so to speak.

Now that she has her own place, she was free to do what she wanted, when she wanted and how she wanted, while preying on the weaknesses of men. She claimed that men were weak, especially if they are married and lonely. She said that she would find her victims by befriending their wives. Tiffany would find out the weaknesses of a person's home by having the wife to confide in her, and then she would track down the husband to befriend him as well. She would find out all of his dirt and record their phone calls to blackmail him into having an affair. Of course, her scheme did not work all the time, but she had a good success rate—she was getting what she wanted. However, if she did not get what she wanted, she would go to her big file cabinet. She would pull out her ammunition to create confusion, spreading all of their dirt to break up their home.

Tiffany was ruthless; but, she knew the rules of the game; therefore, she did not bring a woman around her man PERIOD! She did not care if it was her mom, sister, relative, or friend— nobody came to her house, and she would not take her man to another woman's house. While her conscience became her ultimate guide, she did not trust a woman at all; therefore, she did not have many friends. In my opinion, this was her way of subconsciously protecting herself from being hurt, losing her man to another woman, or to offset her karma, to say the least. As she told me this story, I could only think about this one scripture, "So as a man thinketh in his heart, so is he." She was actually trying to protect herself from becoming a victim of her own schemes; therefore, she could never get out of her own way. As a result, she created her environment based totally on her perception of how she viewed herself, as well as her past that eventually gave birth to her reality.

As Tiffany became a little older and wiser, she decided to settle down after meeting Wallace. He was an intelligent, retired military man who has been around the world and back again. He firmly believes that there is nothing new under the sun—so Tiffany's little mind games did not faze him at all. Actually, he set booby traps for her, because he knew that she would snoop through his things like a typical woman. The more she snooped, the more he played with her mind. Tiffany's little snooping games began to backfire on her mentally. Even though she did not confront him about what she was finding; however, her conversations began to give her away. Wallace knew that he had to teach her a lesson for violating his privacy and the privacy of others.

A few months later, Wallace went out of town, and she stayed up all night trying to dig up dirt on him to figure out where he was going or who he was going with—she found nothing. This began to drive her insane, so she gathered up enough nerves to break into his house with a key that she duplicated a couple of months back. Tiffany was not the least bit nervous; she walked into his house as if she lived there. She began rummaging through his things, looking for anything that she could use against him. All of a sudden, Wallace puts a gun to her head—he stopped her dead in her tracks. He said, "I should blow your brains out." She began to tremble and cry, pleading for her life. Wallace was so angry that she came into his house without his permission that he almost choked the life out of her. Wallace knew then that he had to get rid of her.

This incident would have caused a normal person to stop snooping, but not Tiffany. After they had broken up, Tiffany continued to dig up dirt on him without his knowledge to hopefully use it against him one day. As she moved on to her next victim, this is where all of her deeds came back to bite her in the butt. Tiffany wanted this new guy named Ben, at all cost. It did not matter what she had to do, who she had to hurt or what information she had to dig up—she had to have this man. Six

Chapter 7 | Madam Oracle

months into the relationship, she broke up his home and two months later, she moves into his house. Tiffany thought that she had met the man of her dreams—he promised her the world and she fell for it. He took her on trips; they went out on the town every weekend, and they just could not get enough of each other.

A year later, something changed. The man of her dreams started to become her worst nightmare. She had met a straight-up womanizing alcoholic who was on the down-low. As long as he was getting what he wanted, he did not care about anything else, and she did not realize this until she was head-over-heels in love with him. For some odd reason, she could not let him go or risk being embarrassed by another failed relationship. As he began to slip through her fingers, she tried to buy his love, and it did work for a few hours—then he was back to his old self again.

Tiffany was at a loss with this guy; she tried using information against him, it did not work. He did not care about anything, he had nothing to lose, and he could care less about what people thought of him. Tiffany's little blackmail schemes did not work with him as he began to drive her crazy, especially when she found homemade pornographic movies of him having sex with overweight women and men. It seemed as if Tiffany had a problem with overweight women—she could not believe that a man would engage in an intimate relationship with a heavy woman. Not only that, she could not believe that he would enjoy having sex with a man as well. These are the two contributing factors that drove her crazy or better yet, suicidal.

As Ben began to find out the truth about Tiffany, he lost all respect for her. He did not realize that he had brought a conniving, blackmailing, backbiting woman into his house. He could not *stand the sight of her, so he avoided her as much as possible. The more he stayed away, the more unstable she became, making herself sick, just to get his attention. She even went to the extreme of getting pregnant; which was a bad idea on her behalf. Ben went crazy; he did not want another child, especially from a woman who was mentally unstable. He felt as if she was trying to trap him and he was not going to allow that to happen. He threatened to sabotage her lawsuit if she did not have an abortion, so she did. This was the straw that broke the camel's back; she began to mix alcohol with her medication trying to commit suicide. Ben did not care; he wanted her out of his house, and he would not even take her to the hospital because of her stupidity. Amazingly, she had to call the ambulance for her own suicide attempt.*

For some odd reason, Tiffany refused to leave this man's house. She used every trick in the book to stay; but Ben had one trick up his sleeve that would drive her away; and, that was another woman. He began to bring other women to the house, and he did not extend any form of respect for her; eventually, she left with her tail between her legs, holding on to the memories of what would never be.

The act of being observant is one thing, but plain old snooping is another. The violation of privacy is abusive, and there is no excuse for snooping without permission with a person that is of age. Regardless of where we are in life, we must do our homework on the people, places, and things in our lives. Yes, we must get the facts; however, it's not necessary to violate the privacy of anyone or snoop. Simply ask fact-finding questions.

Chapter 7 | Madam Oracle

And yes, I do agree that we must know who or what we are dealing with, and we must also know who or what we will not deal with. Living by this principle will help us not to settle for people, places, and things that we cannot or choose not to deal with. Our best bet is to get all the details or information before we commit to a person, place, thing, or event. However, if we have to violate the privacy of someone or create an abusive situation to get it, then more than likely that's not the ideal person, place, or thing for us.

As for snooping Tiffany, she moved on with her life, but her health began to fail dramatically due to the extended use and abuse of her pain medications and sleeping pills. Not only that, she now has an incurable STD that she contracted from Ben, and can no longer have unprotected sex with another man. To add insult to injury, she has been diagnosed as a paranoid schizophrenic. She thinks that everyone is out to get her—she is constantly paranoid about someone watching her, tapping her phone, or getting her personal information. Tiffany never realized that her snooping would become her ultimate downfall. Tiffany is now in a mental institution where she's able to receive help for her condition because she refused to use "The Guarded Psalms of Prayer" to help her through her situation.

Does our perception really create our reality?" The answer is no; however, it does influence our reality. It is our self-talk, our ability to refocus, and our thinking process that create our reality. Our perception is used as a tool to positively or negatively influence our thoughts and actions. Therefore, if we use our perception as a positive tool of understanding to become better, stronger and wiser, we would find that our perception will begin to work for us and not against us. In order to survive in the real world, there are 2 things that we must possess, and that is respect and discipline. We will find that our unparalleled sacrifices are usually made in the areas in which we lack discipline or the areas that we lack respect.

Prayer

My Father which art in Heaven, in the Mighty Name of Jesus, I come before You today seeking Divine Direction. I do not know which way to turn, I am lost— please do not allow me to fall by the wayside, because You know the way that I should go, and the way that I should not go. I trust You to go before me, and stand behind me in all that I do, say, and become. Father, for I know if the breadcrumbs fall from the table to the dogs, I know beyond a shadow of a doubt, You will leave breadcrumbs for me to ensure that I can find my way through this jungle of life.

Lord, I surrender all to You, as I follow Your lead with the instinctual nudges that You have given me. I know that if I follow You, I will not be brought to a state of confusion that will contradict Your righteousness. From this day forward, I declare and decree that You deliver me from the hands of the wicked, the hands of the unjustified, the hands of the unrighteous, the hands of the cruel, the hands of the jealous, the hands of the wayward, and the hands of the dream-killers who are trying to control me and my life to cater to his or her selfish ways, dreams, or goals. And, most of all, help me to get out of my own way, in the Mighty Name of Jesus.

As the deep calleth unto the deep, I invoke the presence of the Holy Spirit in my life to allow me to become one with You, Your Will, and Your Way. Father, let nothing or no one separate me from the love that You have for me, and the love that I have for You. Although, I know that my flesh is weak; but Lord, my God, my spirit is willing. Yes, willing to become directed by You, willing to serve You, willing to walk in Your Will and Your Ways—I am Your vessel, mold me in a way that the nay-sayers will witness Your presence in my life; therefore, becoming a living testimony of Your grace and mercy that will draw them unto You. In Jesus' Name, I pray. Amen. Thank you.

Scripture Reading:

Psalms 7
Psalms 10
Psalms 12
Psalms 40
Psalms 51

CHAPTER 8

Guarded Monopoly

We have tons of books on the market telling us how to master the game of love, how to do this and how to do that; but let me say this, there is a difference between playing games, following the rules, and exercising common sense. Tit for tat games will cause us to play ourselves in the end, due to the fact that it causes us to lose our credibility. Once our credibility is lost, it is hard to regain, especially when we are exchanging lies and half-truths. Besides, the last thing that we would ever want to do is to have someone to give up on us because we are playing too many games or have someone to stop believing in us.

"The Guarded Psalms of Prayer" says that the game of love is such a delicate game that we should not run the risk of playing with someone's feelings. This leaves room

for someone to get hurt, and hurting someone out of mere selfishness will cause this game to eventually backfire. It may not come back at that moment, but the Law of Karma is in full effect; therefore, one must tread very carefully when classifying oneself as a PLAYER. Trust that the games we play, will play out; plus, there is someone out there that can play our game better than us, and win at it as well. Therefore, it is better to play by the rules such as Godly principles to ensure that one stays on the winning end of the spectrum, even if it appears as if we are on the losing end.

There are times when it's the CHASE that gets a woman or a man in a relationship—we do not want someone that is such an EASY catch, that anyone can get! During the chase, some of us use game playing as our point of leverage to get a particular individual of interest. But I must say that if we are going to play games to get someone—we must have enough game to keep them. In my opinion, we can get into as many relationships as we so desire, but if we are not able to keep a relationship together after the catch, then what? Now the question is, "What do we do when the game is over, and our catch is now on our back, driving us crazy?" Do we move on to another game? Do we continue the same cycle? Or, do we learn how to tighten up our game?

When we start playing games in a relationship, we will soon find that there is an onset of increased arguments. In the game of life, we all have a desire to win; however, in a relationship, when games are being played, the rules change on a moment-by-moment basis depending on who is winning and who is getting hurt. When this begins to happen, we will find that we will begin to feel like enemies battling for territories of the heart. Incidentally, waiting for the next punchline or who is going to win at a particular game, the couple then ceases to enjoy the relationship or each other, to say the least.

When we have to stay on guard with our emotions with someone that we are trying to trust with our heart, it is not a comfortable feeling; therefore, leaving room for trust issues to surface. This is a level of immaturity that will eventually cause some sort of defeat; if not now, give it some time—the game will backfire because when we become opponents in a relationship, we do not fight fair! In my opinion, this is the deal breaker in a relationship and due to this downfall or breakdown—it is best to part ways before continuing on this path of destruction.

If this type of relationship is continued, the arguments will increase; especially about power, money, sex, the children....name it, arguments will happen. Make no mistake about it, having an argument with our partner or spouse is not a reason to part ways. But having arguments due to constantly playing mind-games with our partner that's resulting in harbored bitterness, anger, or rage that has led up to some form of abuse is definitely a reason to draw a line in the sand on that relationship unless one changes his or her behavior.

Monopolizing Truth

Spiritual monopoly has been around since the beginning of time, and it's not going anywhere anytime soon. For that reason, in all honesty, everyone has their price; which leads me to the question, "Is there a prostitute in every woman and man?" Most would say no; but, I say, "YES." If you are adamant about not having an inner prostitute, then there is definitely a pimp from within. Let me explain; there is temptation in everyone whether we admit it or not.

We are conditioned to think that all prostitutes are on the street corners or in the strip clubs; however, I beg to differ. There are unregulated pimps and prostitutes all around us; actually, the best pimps and prostitutes are not on the streets—they live among us, next door to us, and sometimes within us. Am I calling you a prostitute or pimp? No. I am not calling anyone a prostitute or pimp—I am only bringing about awareness from within.

My friend, whether we are the prostitute, prostituter, pimp, or pimper, our human nature causes us to gravitate to the men and women who possess money, power, or fame, and stray away from those who have little or nothing to offer; therefore, causing 7 things to happen:

1. Spiritual, mental, emotional, physical, and financial prostitution.
2. Pride of Life.

3. Gold Digging.
4. Brown Nosing.
5. Using sex as leverage in a relationship.
6. Buying your way through life.
7. Manipulation and Control of the weak by mental, physical, emotional, spiritual, or financial enslavement.

Are they not all forms of prostitution? Wherever you find idolatry, you will find prostitution! Of course, we would not use the word prostitution, because it's not a politically correct word to use when we are selling our souls in exchange for material and personal gain. We experience it on the job, where most of the mental prostitution and brown nosing takes place. We experience it in the church, where spiritual prostitution is at its best. We experience it in our relationships and in our homes, where the gold digging or sexual leverage takes place. IT IS EVERYWHERE, but not limited to these certain places!

I remember at a very young age; I had a deep infatuation with fancy, sporty cars—my father would always say to me, "Do not go crazy over fancy cars, because you do not know what they had to do to get it." As a child, I did not grasp the true meaning of what he was saying; but, as an adult with a little experience under my belt—I understand. Some go about getting what they want the right way, and some get things the wrong way—who am I to judge? Everyone has done something that they are not proud of at some point.

In order to find out about the pimping prostitute from within, just honestly ask yourself 2 questions:

1. Can I truly be happy with who I am without money?
2. Can I truly be happy with who I am with money?

The first question creates the prostitute from within and the second question creates the pimp from within. If left unchecked, lack creates desperation igniting the prostituting spirit and over-abundance creates arrogance igniting the pimping spirit. Is it the same for everyone? Yes. We will all have the thoughts, but we all will not act upon the thoughts or the temptations of the prostituting or pimping spirit. Thoughts come and go—the pimp or prostitute from within does not make it to reality until we act upon our thoughts. Yes, when we take action— that changes the rules of this game. The more we indulge, the easier it becomes until it is second nature.

Materialism at Its Finest

Materialism has become a plague. When a person enters into a relationship for personal gain, they are considered a gold digger. It's time out for pretending! For example: What do you call a wife who withholds sex because her husband quit his job, forgot her birthday, or took her to McDonalds for their anniversary? An angry wife, right! If the truth were to be told, love runs out real quick when our money starts to look funny, right? We do not want to hear about our motives of silent prostitution, because reality hurts.

A person with a gold-digging mentality is nothing more than a prostitute on the down-low, and a Sugar Daddy or Sugar Momma is nothing more than a pimp on the down-low. Men are taking care of women and women (Cougars) are taking care of men. What about the innocent individuals who have a desire for true love? Is it a thing of the past? Maybe or maybe not!

To my amazement, I have found that we have just as many gold digging males as we do females. Everyone wants something whether we admit it or not—this may include financial support, emotional support, a do-boy, a slave, and the list goes on. We have our own reasons, wants, and desires on why we do what we do, and do not do what we need to do. Let me clear this up; there is nothing wrong with being concerned about your own financial security; however, a gold digger's ultimate goal is financial security from someone other than self. They use fake emotions to gain the trust of their victims and then use them for material gain. This epidemic of material gain has caused countless divorces and breakups due to the loss of a job or business. The marriage vow, *"For better or for worse"* does not mean a thing to a gold digger—they are in the relationship only for the money, when it's gone, they are too. If we are asking or being asked these questions like:

1. Where do you live?
2. Do you own your home?
3. What do you do for a living?
4. How much do you make a year?
5. How many children do you have?

These are questions to determine our net worth or the type of lifestyle that we are accustomed to. These are also the questions that provoke the prostitute or pimp from within.

In order to see if a person is interested in you, delay answering these types of questions. Instead, tell them about you as an individual and the things you like to do—if they are interested, they will ask questions to find out more about you as a person. If they do not, you will automatically know that they are only interested in you for the money or sex. The less you tell a gold digger, the easier it becomes to weed them out. It's imperative that you take a little time to observe their behavior and conversations. However, if your goal is to be a "Sugar Daddy or Sugar Momma" then this does not apply to you, but if you are looking for someone to love you for you, then keep reading.

The top 2 reasons for most divorces is 1. Communication. 2. Money. If the communication is not there, flee. And if you feel as if a person is only around you for the money, flee; or you will set yourself up to become a statistic.

Chapter 8 | Madam Oracle

How to spot a user or gold digger:

1. He or she cannot keep a job.
2. Everything is always someone else's fault.
3. He or she only calls you when they need something.
4. He or she will always talk about himself or herself.
5. His or her conversation changes when they need something. (baby talk, sexy talk, etc.)
6. He or she is very materialistic.
7. He or she has champagne taste on a beer budget.
8. He or she gets angry when they do not receive a gift from you.
9. He or she only has sex with you when you buy them something.
10. He or she makes you pay for everything and never buys you anything.

When the key to a person's heart is through money—is there a difference between people who exchange sex for money? The answer is "NO." There is no difference.

Be True to Thyself

When it comes down to telling the truth about the prostitute from within, we will find that we tend to shy away from being honest with ourselves. Here is one young lady that knows about this all too well, *Respect and discipline were instilled in Megan at a very young age, and she was* proud to be a very respectful and polite woman with certain values and standards. However, Megan had a few flaws which caused her to become insecure. She was able to hide her insecurity most of the time by staying to herself. Although she was a very smart little girl, her flaws made her feel inferior to those who appeared not to have any flaws at all.

Her first step of discipline came when she started reading the Bible every day. She did not become self-confident overnight, but her discipline paid off quite well. Today, this woman is so well-spoken; it's unbelievable how her respect and discipline enabled her to top the charts with her written and spoken words of wisdom. However, along with her wisdom, came her greatest test— POWER, MONEY, AND SEX.

Megan hit a fork in the road with her business. It began to fail while she did almost everything to keep it afloat. The economy put her in a position where she began to lose money—she had great ideas, a great plan, great marketing, great everything, but no money to finance it. The economy put Megan between a rock and a hard place; she could not believe that God would bless her so much, only to lose it like that.

As Megan began to change gears to keep her business running, she would encounter a lot of people who were willing to help her, but there was a catch. They wanted something that violated Megan's will. They had a bargaining tool that made it very tempting for Megan—this one guy Luke, offered to bring her out of the hole with her business if she would become his woman. She thought about it, and she said, "That's not a bad deal." So she began to go out with him. On the 3rd date, he began to touch her in a way that made her feel uncomfortable, as she began to move away, he began to push her head down between his legs. Megan resisted, but she could not believe that she let her guard down, only to become Luke's next freak. So she spoke up, saying, "I am not your prostitute!" He said, "You need something, and I need something, so we are even. Give me what I want and I'll give you what you want." The smirk on his face instantly turned Megan off; therefore, she ended the date, jumped into her car and went home. She realized at that point that he only wanted sex from her and not to really help her. Luke called her for months; she would not take his call—she thought that he was disgusting, and she wasn't willing to lose her soul just to have him save her business. She would rather lose everything, than to give Luke the satisfaction of saying that she had to prostitute herself for something that God has blessed her with.

Megan lost all of her friends during this time of drought, no one came around, no one offered her any help—she was all alone questioning God. As money got really low for Megan, she was short a few dollars on her light bill; she asked a long lost friend of hers for help, but he just gave her the run-around. When she finally caught up with him, he asked her, "What are you going to give me if I help you?" She said, "I will pay you back!" He said, "That's not what I want." She said, "I am not giving it up; I would rather sit in the dark before I allow you to violate my integrity." He said, "Okay, sit in the dark. You will be back." Megan could not believe that her long-time friend wanted to break her down, in her time of need. Although God made a way for her, she cried all night long. Her heart wasn't broken because of not having the money to pay the light bill; her heart was broken *because, in her time of weakness, her friend tried to take advantage of her and the situation.*

Megan did not settle for the sexual, economic or emotional abuse that was placed before her—she was determined to use *"The Guarded Psalms of Prayer"* to find her way into greatness. As a result, Megan eliminated all of the so-called friends that mistreated or used her during her time of famine. She did not lose her company; actually, her integrity saved it—her company became a multi-million dollar empire. Megan learned that insecurities are designed to drive greatness out of us regardless of how it may seem at the time.

Insecurity is basically an obstruction or hindrance that will create a superficial image of weakness. When a weakness is exposed to others; most often, we retreat out of shame instead of taking our weakness and turning it into something great. A weakness exposed is better than a weakness covered up; as a matter of fact, an exposed weakness will give us more of an incentive to work on that area; but on the other hand, when our weakness is covered up, it is easier to overlook or make excuses for it. The truth is, we all have some form of an impediment. Some are able to cover them up better than others; but in all reality, we all fall short in some area of our lives! However, this is not the time to worry about falling short or being perfect! For that reason, Megan understands that there is cause and effect all around us. However, when we try to change the rules of the game by fighting the effect and not the cause, then we can pretty much expect disarray and disorder to take place in our lives. When we become selfish about having things our way, we will find that we limit the way in which we are able to excel, especially when the feeling of negative déjà vu is involved.

When déjà vu presents itself in your life, that's your cue to embrace the opportunity to do things better by enhancing what you are not doing or curtailing what you are doing. Finding the cause of something can and will give you better leverage over the effects in your life. Just remember, an impediment cannot keep you blocked if you look for the benefit. When you do that, greatness is inevitable creating an open door of opportunity for you to take advantage of. Today, take a look at the timeline of your life to see what's repeating itself and why. The image that we hold of ourselves will determine whether we are going to become a survivor or prey.

Megan enabled herself to become faithfully and meekfully interdependent, allowing everyone to play his or her role in her life. She mysteriously found that when nothing else seems to work, her faithful interdependence with her Heavenly Father would! It was through her faith and meekness that attracted that one idea, that one thought, that one reaction, that one whatever…. that changed her life forever. Megan is a true survivor, and she teaches others to embrace their true value as well. Megan's trust handed her a meekness that people could not understand. This woman has a way of humbling herself to elevate others into divine greatness. She does not pretend to be better than anyone else; she makes it her business to present herself like a humble child to find the diamonds in the ruff. She understood that if she appreciated life, it would make her survival a little easier. She said that the best way to survive a situation or circumstance in life is to appreciate it.

I must agree, money can buy most of what we want, but it cannot always buy what we need. When I was on my deathbed several years ago, and I was the youngest person in the Intensive Care Unit. The doctors said that I was in bad shape, but I knew that I was in that unit for a reason. So I decided to talk with the older men and women there, asking them one important question, "If you could rewrite your life, what would you do differently?" They all said, "Spend more time with my family." I never heard anyone speak about money, a job, or material wealth—they only spoke about family. I thought that was so amazing to spend years attaining and the last years wishing that they could have enjoyed the one thing that they neglected.

Money cannot buy love, peace, happiness, sanity, integrity, or freedom—it comes from within. Let me close this chapter with one of my favorite scriptures from Isaiah 55:1-2. It says, *"Ho, every one that thirsteth, come ye to the waters, and he that hath no money; come ye, buy, and eat; yea, come, buy wine and milk without money and without price. Why do you spend money for that which is not bread? and your labor for that which satisfies not? Listen diligently to me, and*

Chapter 8 | Madam Oracle

eat you that which is good, and let your soul delight itself in fatness." Take your time; it's not about the money, it's about what you possess from within. Our spiritual development is imperative to conquer the temptations that are designed to sift us.

Prayer

My Father, which art in Heaven, it is You that I worship, it is You that I give homage to; besides You, there is no other. I humbly admit that the greatness of my soul resides within You. O' Lord, it is through Your grace and mercy that I am still standing. It is through You, that I am able to let go of the past, for it is already gone, I don't need it anymore. It is through You that I am able to reserve that space for the more positive, productive, and fruitful aspects of greater things.

Father, You said in Your Word, "Greater is in me, than he who's in the world." For that reason, I am choosing the Greater, as I make it my business to claim victory on a daily basis, I am owning it; because, I know that You will not withhold any good thing from me. By the Blood of Jesus, even when life doesn't appear victorious in my sight—open my Spiritual Eyes to see the greater, and the more positive aspects that my natural eyes cannot see. This will ensure that the spirit of deception does not come in to taint my thoughts, sifting me in an unproductive direction. I know that Greatness is in my Bloodline; therefore, I declare and decree, that

You push back my known and unknown enemies or issues that may try to thwart my greatness from coming forth. For that reason, my God, I pray that You cover my nakedness, to ensure that the shame of my previous mistakes and misbehaviors do not become a hindrance to my success, in the Name of Jesus.

Father, I know that everything that I need is already within me; and everything that I desire, I need to find it within You first—this will ensure that I keep Your divine order intact. You said in Your Word, "Seek Ye first the Kingdom of God, and His righteousness; and all these things will be added to me." Now, with that being said, I am seeking Your face through praise, worship, and prayer to ensure that the floodgates of my greatness come from Your hand, with no sorrow attached to it.

Greatness is my birthright, in the Name of Jesus. On this day, I lay claim to the birthright that has been passed down to me from my Forefathers, Abraham, Isaac, and Jacob—I am here to claim my inheritance in Christ Jesus as I pull down any strongholds that have been waged against me, or the greatness that lies within the depths of my soul. For this, O' Lord, I give thanks to You as I claim greatness right now. In the Name of Jesus. Thank you. Amen.

Scripture Reading:
Psalms 1
Psalms 14

Chapter 8 | Madam Oracle

Psalms 21
Psalms 30
Psalms 45
Psalms 50
Psalms 87
Psalms 108

CHAPTER 9

Guarded Soul

The Power of Love and Freedom can sometimes become very fearful; but at the same time, it can become very empowering as well. Throughout my years of love and freedom, as well as the lack of it; what I have found is that in order to make love work for us, we must set limits, boundaries, and expectations in a relationship by following certain Godly Rules and Principles.

If we do not, we will fall for anything….and, falling for anything is not a Godly characteristic for those who are designed to soar like eagles. As we already know, the DO-IT-YOURSELF relationships only work temporarily without the Wisdom of God or the Mind of Mastery. Therefore, it is imperative that we learn how to incorporate Godly principles, at the beginning of the relationship to ensure that we do not have to backtrack, undo, or redo things that we can get right the first time around.

In order to live a life of favorable love, we must take into account certain rules or criteria's for successful living to build our very own framework or our version of love. Love can very well mean something different for each of us; however, I am going to lay the groundwork to ensure that we are equipped with the basic fundamental elements of love to ensure that we do not fall by the wayside, even if we somehow get caught up in loving someone that does not love us back. Here are the 21 Mind of Mastery Godly Rules—this is indeed the GAME CHANGING POWER that we need to succeed in any relationship:

I am going to get started with Rule #1: *"Run from sexual sin. No other sin affects the body as this one"* 1 Corinthians 6:18. Of course, no one wants to hear about this rule—it is indeed the hardest one to abide by, but it is the most crucial one. This is the #1 reason why we have problems in our love life....yes, sexual immorality is asking for trouble. We cannot think for a minute that we can indulge in this sinful behavior and live in total peace—it's not going to happen like that! We will have trials and tribulations in this area—it is to be expected!

Make no mistake about it, if we take a moment to look around us, emotional scarring is out of control, sexual diseases are out of control, promiscuity is out of control, we are hooking up with mere strangers over the

Chapter 9 | Madam Oracle

internet—are we not destroying ourselves? Are we not creating our own bed of hurt, betrayal, and confusion? These are some of the questions that we must ask ourselves when dealing with our sexuality and love.

As the Bible says *"Do not give to the dogs what's holy, or cast your pearls among the swine"* Matthew 7:6. As a part of our spiritual understanding, this brings me to Rule #2: We must be mindful of who occupies our time. It is a proven fact that we become who we hang around with; therefore, we must become ever so cognizant of the people who we are breaking bread with.

Do you think for a minute we can sit in the presence of fools all the time, and expect wisdom to flow from our loins? We will never see Eagles on the ground with Chickens…the day that we do, something is wrong! We will never see a Lion, the King of the Jungle, hanging out with Turtles, the day that we do, something is wrong! Proverb 13:20 says, *"If we hang with the wise and we become wise, but we will suffer if we hang around fools."* Therefore, we must select our environment carefully, because the wrong choice could become detrimental to our mental, physical, emotional, and spiritual well-being.

Trust that when people are broken down, they will subconsciously try to break others down as well; therefore, we must become very careful about our influences, as well as who is speaking over our lives. It is also imperative that we "Do not become unequally yoked" with those who are going in a totally different direction….if sex is all that a couple has in common, that should be the writing on the wall!

Rule #3: We must be mindful about who we open our hearts to *"For out of the abundance of the heart springs the issues of life"* Proverbs 4:23. Before I move on, as a Word of Wisdom, if we cannot trust someone to tell the truth or they trust us more with their lies than their truths, then why should we trust them with our hearts? Therefore, if this is the case with anyone, we must make sure that we set a guard over our heart to ensure that we do not set a trap for ourselves.

This is where we need to weed out the Deceptive Spirits—these are the people who are trying to prey on our weaknesses to benefit themselves. If one feels used or abused early in a relationship, BAIL OUT! Do not wait, this sort of behavior gets worse; and if we are looking to change someone, then stop looking. We are not in the business to raise grown people; if a person wants to treat us right, they will. We do not have to force them! If a person wants to love us unconditionally, they will. We do not have to force them. If a person wants to be faithful to us, they will. We do not have to force them.

Point in fact, we cannot change people, we can only change ourselves, while providing a safety zone of understanding and patience for others to change, if they desire to do so. If not, we are fighting a losing battle because "change" is the prerequisite for living a fulfilled

Chapter 9 | *Madam Oracle*

lifestyle. And, if someone is resistant to change, then leave them alone and focus on that in which is positive, productive, and fruitful.

Rule #4: We must play our role in a relationship. We are designed to be independent, and able to stand on our own two feet and love ourselves. We are also designed to become interdependent in a relationship, being able to work together with others to achieve a common goal.

Nevertheless, God has set a certain order in place—when a man is playing the woman's role in the household, there is disorder. When a woman is playing a man's role in a relationship, there is disorder. When children are running the household, there is disorder, etc. Of course, everyone will have their own set of rules when it comes down to their lives; but, there is a whole new ball game when it comes down to living a loving Godly lifestyle—we must follow Divine Order.

The man is the head of the household, and the woman is his helpmeet; in Genesis 2:18 it says *"It's not good that man should be alone; I will make a helpmeet for him."* If the man is not providing a spiritual covering for his house, they will experience turmoil. If he is not making provisions for his house, there will be turmoil. If he is not leading his house, there will be turmoil. Being the head of the house is not designed for him to abuse his role in a relationship; it's designed for him to take RESPONSIBILITY for his house, to set order in his house as it should be, to protect his house, and follow the other rules regarding love.

For all the single women that do not have a man as of yet, and must play the man and the woman's role, it is okay to be that Proverb's 31 woman, handling everything. But when she gets a man, husband or whatever, it is imperative that she dethrones herself; meaning she must relinquish her power to allow the man to become the head of the household. If not, she will tear down her very own house with her bare hands. Believe it or not, this is where the love/hate relationships come into play, and this is exactly why 80% of marriages are ending in divorce.

Power struggles between a man and a woman in a relationship go against Godly principles, regardless of how we view this woman's liberation thing. Let me clear this up and make it real simple, for as long as singleness hovers over a woman's life; she is liberated! But as soon as she says, "I DO" to him, she gives up that freedom to help meet his needs, the needs of the family, and the needs of the UNION, COMMON GOAL, or PURPOSE of the relationship. If this does not happen, the married woman or man will feel alone or single, which puts a relationship at risk of extramarital affairs to fill that little void that they cannot tell their spouse about. We can play house all we want, but this is real life; and when it comes down to LOVE, Godly principles apply to us all, regardless of our deed or creed.

Rule #5: Exercise obedience in a relationship. When we talk about being or becoming obedient, most people cringe at this word. However, before I go any further with this subject, let me say this, I am not referring to physical abuse here. If a woman or her children are in danger, she must do something about it—her safety and the safety of her family should be her number 1 priority.

Now, that we have that out of the way, obedience, in my opinion, it is one of the most powerful attributes in a loving relationship. If we are not able to listen and obey our partner or spouse, then we become divided; and a divided house cannot stand! This does not make a woman a servant to her husband; it makes her want to CATER to her husband as she should.

When we are able to cater to people out of mere loving and obedient servanthood, we are able to open the door to spiritual empowerment on a level that selfish individuals will never understand. This is another SECRET that goes overlooked time and time again—in order to lead our field in any area of our lives, we must be willing to serve wholeheartedly with a positive mental attitude.

When a man cannot listen to his woman, there is a DISCONNECT, and there will be problems in the relationship. When a woman cannot listen to her man, there is a DISCONNECT, and there will be problems in the relationship. This is a BIG warning sign when embarking into a relationship with someone. If they outright go against everything that is being said, one must realize that they are dealing with a Confrontational Jezebel Spirit. This is a controlling spirit that breaks down a person in ways that they will not be able to recover; therefore, we must exercise extreme caution when dealing with an individual who prides themselves on being disobedient.

We can look for any reason to justify our behavior in a relationship, and we can also create any reason to justify us getting out of the relationship as well. But if we have intentionally instigated havoc in our relationship, do we think for a minute that God is interested in our happiness? If we have intentionally brought contention in our home through our acts of disobedience, do we think that God is interested in our feelings?

It amazes me that we are praying to God about a bad marriage, but we are not submissive to our husband or wives, and we are tearing down our house with our bare hands....is that a double standard? And, we want God to listen to us, when we have developed a deaf ear to our husband or wife. I am not posing these questions to bash anyone; I am posing them to get us to thinking about some of our blocked prayers, as well as some of our blocked blessings.

As a Word of Wisdom, before we take our marriage, our relationship, our family, our friendship, etc. to God, it is always best to line ourselves and our relationships up with scripture or Godly principles first. We cannot expect God to uphold our wayward behavior just because we got our feelings hurt....a marriage, a relationship, a family, a friendship, etc. takes work, and we cannot bail out anytime we feel like it; especially if we are exhibiting unrectified bossy, quarrelsome, or belligerent behavior.

Rule #6: This is by far the Golden Rule: *"Do unto others as you would have them do unto you."* Luke 6:31. If one does not like being mistreated, do not mistreat others. If one has a desire for love, do not withhold love from others. The Law of Reciprocity is in full effect, and God cannot be mocked because *"We will reap what we sow"* according to Galatians 6:7. Therefore, if we think that we are getting away with our wayward behavior, think again! In due season, it will catch up with us; so it is always best to do what's right in the sight of God, to ensure that goodness will always come back when the time is right.

The way in which we treat God, ourselves, our spouse, our children, and others can indeed hinder our prayers. Therefore, if we find ourselves blocked in a certain area of our lives, we must quickly try to pinpoint where we went wrong; and I personally, evaluate my attitude and behaviors first. I firmly believe that we must give love, honor, and respect to all; and if we are treating a stranger better than we are treating our loved ones, then we are definitely out of order. This brings me to this one story: *I ran into this woman some time ago, and her child was having a hard time financially because she was in recovery from a major illness. She saw that her child was losing a lot of* weight, and the woman blew it off as if her child was on some sort of diet. Then one day her child could not take the hunger pains anymore; therefore, she swallowed her pride, and she asked her mom for something to eat. Her mom gave her a piece of meat and a soda to drink. Some people would take this as an insult, but this child was hungry, and she was grateful for whatever was given to her.

A week later, upon her routine visit to her mom's house; she noticed that her mom was trying to get rid of her quickly; therefore, she started asking questions about why her mom was trying to get rid of her. The mom then says that she was taking someone out to dinner—this child felt so hurt because she had nothing to eat all day. The mother that she loves so much is feeding someone else's child without even extending any sort of invitation to feed her own. Although very hurt, this child did not form any resentment, she still loved and helped her mom with no strings attached. Nevertheless, she stopped asking for food, and placed her needs in the hands of God.

The following week after the incident, this child was helping her mom without having one morsel of food in her belly—she did not say a word to anyone about it, she just continued to do a good deed for her mother. Then a stranger walks up, and offers to help her; then she realizes that the stranger was not really a stranger, she had met him before. This person then offers to buy her some food; she said that she would accept on one condition—he had to buy food for her mom as well. He gladly accepts, and the mother felt so embarrassed about the incident, she hung her head down in shame. However, the mom does offer to feed her child later on that day without her daughter having to ask for food.

Chapter 9 | Madam Oracle

Is this an atrocity? Maybe or maybe not….this woman's child placed her faith in God, and He not only provided a meal for this child at that moment, but He also gave her a husband as well. He was the man of her dreams….he was that child's BOAZ….this child never had to go hungry another day in her life. She could not ask for a better man; he loves her in a way that no man has ever loved her.

It was not about the hunger or the meal; it was about this child's faith meeting up with her famine. The only way that this child could get to her blessing was through her mom's atrocious behavior. As life would have it, the love that this child displayed in spite of disappointments was her blessing in disguise; even when people looking from the outside in thought otherwise because she was hungry and had to live through her famine.

There is no possible way that we can think that God is going to rain down bountiful blessings on those who are treating people like a junkyard dog or hurting innocent people—we have to check and see where those superficial blessings are really coming from! No one and I mean no one can convince me otherwise on that one….God is a God of Love. And if one is prospering in hatefulness or ruthlessness, it very well may not be a blessing; it may be a curse in disguise. Therefore, we must exercise extreme caution regarding how we treat others; we never want to curse our own hand with our wayward behavior.

The Guarded Psalms of Prayer   123

Rule #7: *"Our honor is to avoid strife and confusion"* Proverbs 20:3. We must feel SAFE in a relationship—SAFE mentally, emotionally, physically, spiritually, and financially. If we say that we love someone, it means that we do not have to fuss or fight with them to prove our love for them. Hitting, yelling, screaming, fussing, or fighting with someone exhibits a lack of self-control; therefore, if we have a desire to maintain our dignity, we must walk away. Love does not make us live like this; it is the desire for control that provokes us to live in such a manner. If our attitude and behavior are causing tension in the family, problems on the job, problems in a relationship, or some sort of emotional trauma, it is a possibility that one must consider reevaluating his or her attitude and behavior.

It is Satan's job to kill, steal, and destroy our homes—if we are too busy fussing, fighting, plotting our revenge, and licking our wounds, we do not have time protecting ourselves and our family from the vicious wiles of the enemy. It is best to save that time and energy for things that are positive, productive, and fruitful. Our homes should be our Zone of Safety, and if we are not able to feel safe in our home, in a relationship, or with our family, we will find a place to rest our head. And, God forbid that we rest our head in the wrong place. That place can be with another person; it can be an addiction; it can be anything that causes us to feel loved, even if it's temporary.

Rule #8: *"A house divided against itself cannot stand."* (Mark 3:25). What goes on in the house, stays in the house. When we broadcast our family affairs, instead of it being family business, it becomes everyone's business. This leaves room for everyone to begin to run our household, which is out of order. When we have too many heads in our house, we will find that chaos and confusion will supersede the peace in one's house. Therefore, public humiliation is off limits—we always conduct our affairs in private.

Rule #9: *"Reflect the character of Christ in all that you do."* (Galatians 2:20). It is best to think about our behavior and how we conduct ourselves on a moment-by-moment basis. Whenever we are out in public, we are a representative of our home training....regardless of whether it's the big or the little simple things in life. It is imperative that we live our lives like there is a camera watching us at all times. When we allow our conscience to become our guide, there are a lot of things that we are not going to do.

Rule #10: *"He who covers over an offense promotes love, but whoever repeats the matter separates close friends."* (Proverbs 17:9). There is no need to expose each other's weaknesses to friends and family members—this leaves room for too many opinions and judgments. This type of love protects each other at all cost; I am referring to that "Ride or Die" kind of love. If one does not feel as if this individual has their back, leave them alone. Trust me, if our mate does not have our back, as soon as we let go of their hand, make a mistake, or refuse to stand by their side, they will sell us out, sell us short, or betray us in order to control the relationship. Is this fair? Of course not, but it is the reality that we live in. Simply look around us, there are more married couples airing dirty laundry than those who are mere enemies.

Rule #11: *"The husband must fulfill his duty to his wife, and likewise also the wife to her husband."* (1 Corinthians 7:3) It is always best not to withhold sex from our mate. If we are married, it is our responsibility to keep our mate satisfied—if not, we are definitely out of order.

Rule #12: *"Be kind and gentle, trusting God to work in the heart of the other person."* (2 Timothy 2:24-25). Respect for our mate is of the utmost importance....but, gentleness is even more important! No one wants to be ruffed up—if we treat our mate like a KING, we are on the right path with our Queenship potential. Even if they are not nice, we do not have to stoop to their level—be nice because we are called to do so.

Rule #13: *"Be angry, yet do not sin; do not let the sun go down while you are still angry."* (Ephesians 4:26). Squash whatever it is—when we are sleep, our minds need to be free to prevent an overload of negativity to ensure that we are able to sleep in peace. In my opinion, anger is one letter short of danger; and I personally stay away from individuals who are angry all the time. For me, it's like a time bomb waiting to happen.

Rule #14: *"Do not repay evil with evil."* (Romans 12:17). Leave the tit for tat games for kids. Assume responsibility and resolve conflict with good and not evil. When we sow discord, we will reap it as well. Remember two wrongs do not make it right.

Rule #15: *"Rejoice with the truth."* (1 Corinthians 13:6). Honesty and openness in a relationship are better than a relationship full of lies or half-truths. If we are NOT able to trust our mate with the truth, why would we trust them with a lie?

Rule #16: *"A man who loves his wife loves himself."* (Ephesians 5:28). The level in which we love our mate is a direct reflection on the level in which we love ourselves. A negative self-image stems from real or perceived deprivation of love, rejection, or abuse; therefore, one does not want to relive that again. If we do not know how to love, then we need to LEARN!

Rule # 17: *"A man's honor is to avoid strife."* (Proverbs 20:3). Personal attacks or the blaming game in a relationship are not necessary....if we have to attack the person that we are in relations with, with his or her past issues or contempt, it is best that we move on. Our dignity rides on the line every time we rehash the things of old or disrespect someone….if one cannot get over it, move on.

Rule # 18: *"A gentle answer turns away wrath."* (Proverbs 15:1). We must speak with kindness to our mate, and to all that we come in contact with. Name calling and loud talking are out of the equation, as well as other verbal abuse such as criticizing, belittling, or extreme public humiliation.

Rule #19: *"Let no unwholesome word proceed from your mouth, but only such a word as is good for edification, that it may give grace to those who hear it."* (Ephesians 4:29). We must build up our mate and not tear them down. It is imperative that we avoid mentally, emotionally, physically, and spiritually destructive relationships. And, we must also ensure that we are not creating that type of hostile relationship for others as well. In a relationship, we are designed to empower each other, and if we are not doing that, we are defeating the purpose of why we are truly relating to each other.

Rule #20: *"Where you have envy and selfish ambition, there you find disorder and very evil practice."* (James 3:16). If we have a desire for chaos and confusion NOT to rise up out of our house, it is imperative that we do not COMPARE our mate with other people, especially with an EX. They are our EX's for a reason; whatever that reason is—we are not there! Therefore, leave our EX's out of our present relationship because it is through comparison that we cause envy to bring out bitterness and hatefulness.

Proverbs 3:27 states very clearly, *"Do not withhold good from those who deserve it when it's in your power to help them."* When people are scorned by the way they are treated when they are down and out, they may forgive, but they do not forget! Listen to me, we must be careful about the bridges that we burn, since we never know when we may need to cross that bridge again. Even if we are on top of our game now, it takes a fraction of a second for the game to reverse its role. Plus, it's not a laughing matter when the game is on top of us; therefore, if a couple is not able to work together as a team to achieve a common goal, what makes us think that the relationship can survive with us being arch enemies? Our goal should be to leave a person better off than when we met them, and if we cannot do that, LEAVE THEM ALONE!

Rule #21: *"Greet one another with a kiss of love."* (1 Peter 5:14). We must greet our mate, children, or family member when entering or leaving our homes. It is very rude to walk in or out of the house without extending some form of greeting. This type of behavior creates an ice-cold house, when we should be developing a warm, loving environment. Upon entering the house, when we meet and greet our mate, children, or family member at the door, kiss them, ask them about their well-being, and talk with them for approximately 2-3 minutes to show genuine concern about their day, then we can go about our business as normal. This creates value in the relationship like we would not believe. It does not take long to show that we love and care about them!

When they exit the house, walk them to the door, wish them well, bless them, and tell them to have a good day or be safe....it works! And, if one would try to use the excuse about being at work or too busy, save it—find a way!

Whether we are in the game or playing by the rules, there are a few things that we must know....In order to win at love, we must have the desire to do so; and, we must also have our gratefulness intact as well. If we are not grateful for our successes in love, they will appear as failures due to our mindset. It is imperative that we have a winning attitude in the midst of what appears to be a loss as well. Because there are times when we will not win physically; but, we must win mentally and emotionally to ensure that we are able to create a win-win situation in order to make the appropriate corrections necessary.

In my opinion, becoming a loser or winner in a relationship is basically a mindset—we will win to lose and lose to win to complete the cycle of learning. It is indeed through the process of learning and understanding that we become WISE and LOVEABLE. I will also say this, "It is okay to lose something or someone that's not good for us, or that will drain the life out of us."

We cannot win the heart of everyone all the time, and we will not lose the heart of everyone all the time; however, if we believe that we are a winner at heart, and we perfect those very skills, we will definitely draw more loving people, places, and things than we will lose. As we all know, we attract what we think about all the time, but winning is also a developmental process as well. We cannot sit around talking the game of a winner and not produce the results of a winner. We must work on ourselves every day, set goals, and work toward an end result of winning instead of living our lives like playing lotto or the luck of the draw, expecting great things to happen—real winning does not work like that!

Throughout my journey in and out of the game, I have found that the rules of winning hold the trump card because it is comprised of diligence, humility, compassion, and integrity. Without having these certain characteristics, the game will leave one questioning his or her MOTIVES for the appearance of superficial winning in the end! Manipulating, conniving, scheming, and using people to get what we want are qualities that are NOT conducive to building lasting POWER of a truly winning personality. This type of individual, such as the player personality, quickly breaks the bonds of trust when they are on the losing end; therefore, we must exercise extreme caution when dealing with a person possessing this type of personality.

In order to change the game to make it work in our favor, we must attempt to follow the rules to the best of our ability. We must love like we've never been hurt before giving everyone a clean slate until proven otherwise. We need an awareness of why we are winning. We need an understanding of what it's going to take to win. We must be willing to do everything in the Spirit of Excellence. We need the motivation to win, especially when we want to give up, and we must be willing to pray while trusting the gift from within to supply all our needs.

Real winners will not brag about being a winner or pout over who does not love them. They simply get down to business and make things happen creating a win-win situation out of everything, without settling for defeat from the naysayers who are stuck on negative, stuck on material gain, or stuck on pimping them out to break their focus. It takes Y.O.U. to win—it is just a thought away, so create a win-win situation out of a negative one and do not be afraid to let go of what or who is not drawing out the winner inside of you.

Prayer

I will have what I decree..... I will have whatever I desire, and I will have what God has destined for me, with clean hands and a pure heart. God, You are my point of divine provision, I will not have any want or need in my life that will contradict Your divine purpose. For, I know that it is Your will for me to have prosperity, it is Your will for me to have peace, it is Your will for me to have spiritual purity, and it is Your will for me to have greatness beyond any human imagination. Father, my God, I also know that it is Your will for me to be submerged in good health, strength, sound mind, and stability without any regrets attached to it, in the Name of Jesus.

Henceforth, I declare and decree, that light is brought to the dark areas of my life, as Your word becomes the lamp under my feet, and a light unto my path, O' Lord, my Strength and my Redeemer. Let this light destroy all darkness that's hovering over me, my finances, my mental state of being, my emotional stability, or any area of my life—I break, and destroy all negatives spiritual energies, or forces that are designed to sift me. As the deep calleth unto the deep, I invoke Divine protection, and oneness with the Holy Spirit, as You allow my Guardian Angels to clear my path of all unwanted, negative debris, influences, or obstacles that are designed to sift me as wheat.

By the Spiritual Power that is vested within me, I will have what I decree..... Right now in the Mighty Name of Jesus, I declare and decree that I have good health, blessed wealth, a great attitude, and good success, while my gift makes room for me; therefore, placing me before men in high places with favor beyond all human understanding. As I move forward in Your will and Your way, I am asking that Your peace permeates my life. I know beyond a shadow of a doubt, by placing You first in my life, this will enable me to have a positive mental attitude. By doing so, it will enable me to make good decisions for myself, my career, my home, my family, my relationships, and in my spiritual pursuit of divine greatness, in the Name of Jesus. For it is through Your grace and mercy, my Heavenly Father, that I will have what I decree.....Thank you, and Amen. Amen. Amen.

Scripture Reading:

Psalms 23
Psalms 47
Psalms 103
Psalms 116
Psalms 135

CHAPTER 10

Guarded from Life Irritations

Attitude is everything! A good attitude can help us accomplish anything that we set our mind to do. Values, beliefs, and desires, really control how we behave or react to the people, places, and things around us. Furthermore, what we believe about ourselves becomes evident in our attitude and in our daily living.

Over the years, I have seen a great decline in the importance of having a great attitude. Actually, some people think that it's cool to be rude; in my opinion, a rude person expresses the lack of discipline. For me, everything is based on my attitude towards it—I was taught from an early age that the right mental attitude would pave the way to my future. Low and behold, it has. Now I tell others that the right mental attitude is by far the way to go when you are on top of your game or when your game is on top of you. I firmly believe that a negative attitude really slows down our effectiveness and productivity; therefore, creating poor performance giving us more of a reason to have a positive attitude. Here is a story that is a perfect example of having a desirable attitude:

Sidney has the most ideal attitude; he is the type of person that most people would love to hate or hate to love. He's always in a fabulous mood; actually, he walks around daily encouraging those who could care less about being encouraged. It really seemed as if Sidney never had a bad day. He would always walk around the office saying that he was born to motivate and encourage people. If there was someone going through a tough time, he was able to turn that person's day around without giving it a second thought. To see Sidney in action was like watching Dr. Phil—Sidney did not have a degree, but he was really good. His spiritual approach would put the best atheist in awe. It was so amazing to see how he could change a bad situation into a good one.

I became curious about his technique, so one day I went up to Sidney and asked him, "How do you do it? How can you be so positive and encourage people all the time? What's your secret?" Sidney replied, "There is no secret. It's a choice. Each morning I wake up, I choose to be happy and I, then, ask God to give me my daily bread while allowing me to be a blessing to someone else." He also said, "Each time something bad happens, I can choose to be a victim, or I can choose to learn from it. So, I choose to learn from it and take that lesson and share it with someone else as well." "Yeah, right, it's not that simple," I replied. Then Sidney responded back saying, "Yes, it is, and that's why the simple things in life elude the best of us." He also explained that every time we hear a complaint, just point out the positive and discard the negative. He believes that our life is all about the choices that we make, we can choose to be and have anything.

I still had a hard time believing Sidney, because I thought that he was feeding me a bunch of hype, until one day I heard that he had a heart attack. I went to visit him in the hospital; I instantly began to think positive while praying that he would make it through. When I entered the room, Sidney had a smile on his face. I could not believe that Sidney had something to smile about. As I began to cry, he said, "Wipe away those tears because I am going to make a full recovery and we are going to jog a couple of miles together when I recover."

About four months after the heart attack, he was back to himself. When I asked him how he was doing, he replied. "Attitude is everything, so how about that jog?" After his ordeal, Attitude, after all, was everything.

Sidney did not wait to get a new attitude; he lived it daily. He made a full recovery because he knew beyond a shadow of a doubt that his attitude about life was his everything. It was basically through his attitude that he changed the lives of his onlookers.

I must admit that when the pressure of life weighs you down, it becomes quite challenging to have a great attitude. However, this comes with the territory of challenges when we are dealing with ultimate achievement. It is imperative that we keep a great attitude, even when we are going through a tough time.

The key to our breakthrough is to keep our emotions under control, not allowing negative thoughts to disrupt our peace from within while we:

1. Prepare ourselves daily for the next day.
2. Close the chapter of what has happened in our past, while understanding that it was only a lesson.
3. Take advantage of the present.
4. Exercise patience.
5. Get ready for what is about to happen in our lives.
6. Focus on where we are and where God is taking us.
7. Take action to better ourselves.
8. Position ourselves to be blessed.
9. Move into position.

The driving force of our passion resides in our ability to dedicate ourselves to that in which is destined to challenge us. What I have definitely found in life is that anything or anyone worth having is worth working for. The dynamics of achieving success in anything or with anyone requires us to persevere through our challenges to achieve a common goal. And, whatever that common goal is—is up to us, and it is our responsibility to work toward it with due diligence.

Do you expect the worst out of life or do you expect the best? How often do we have an expectation about a person, place or thing and not realize it? Our expectations are based upon our experiences and self-belief. There are some who are fortunate enough to have all good experiences, as there will always be those who have the not so good experiences as well. Fear of failure and the lack of self-confidence are the enemies that impede the development of our positive expectations. If we fail to make the appropriate changes to counteract the effects of our negative expectations, we will soon find that it becomes extremely hard to move forward and embrace the opportunities that bring about positive change. When the negative critic from within dominates our thoughts, our expectations in life become very doubtful and insecure.

The power of our expectations are governing factors that contribute to our belief system, therefore creating our known or unknown reality. Our beliefs, desires, and expectations have a way of empowering us or causing us to settle for defeat. Here is a story that fits into what I am talking about: *Sissy is said to be a well-known go-getter. Whatever she wants, she puts in the hard work to attain; but she had a little problem called JEALOUSY. She had to deal with her jealous family members who found ways to try to kill her dream and a little copycat sister, who did not have a mind of her own. Sissy's little sister Margaret, never took the time out to find her own dreams, aspirations, and goals in life—she found it more conducive to ride on the coattail of someone else's dreams. Although Sissy did not care about her sister's copycat syndrome, she did have a problem with how her sister treated her. Margaret did not care who she hurts, as long as she got what she wanted, when she wanted it. She used Sissy to the extreme, taking her kindness for a weakness and then talked about her behind her back as if she was the scum of the earth.*

Sissy and Margaret grew up in the same home under 2 different sets of rules—Margaret being the baby of the family was nurtured to the extreme, while Sissy was neglected, and treated like the scum of the earth, or better yet, a slave so to speak. Although that became Sissy's norm, she learned how to deal with her family being nice when they wanted something, and switching out on her when they did not need her. However, that form of treatment did not stop her from loving and helping others. Sissy had to make up her mind to love herself and love others, no matter what. She also made a decision not to make others feel the pain of being neglected, nor would she allow others to kill her dream.

As years continued to roll by, Sissy continued on her pursuit of greatness, as the rest of her family envied her. Sissy learned how to mastermind multiple ways of generating income. She came up with a system to start a lucrative business that made a fair amount of money in her spare time. However, the straw that broke the camel's back is when her conniving sister used her for information to start the same business with the same system; therefore, becoming a direct competitor in the same marketplace. Her sister knew her system and how she did business, which caused her to become duplicatable. For the first time in Sissy's life, she lost her identity of being unique. Everything that she did to change her approach in business, her sister emulated her, and would not let up—when it came down to making money, her sister was ruthless.

Chapter 10 | Madam Oracle

After many months of prayer, God dealt with Sissy's insecurities regarding those who emulated her. From childhood, Sissy had a problem with people copying her; and, if someone copied her, she would give up and do something different. As a matter of fact, Sissy felt as if she had to be the best, smartest, and the greatest at everything—not realizing that it would lead up to the ultimate heartbreak of her life. God allowed Sissy to realize that He did not allow her sister to become her competitor to surpass her—He allowed it to expose a weakness that she had to deal with before He took her to the next level of living. It's amazing how Margaret betrayed her sister for the money, and her sister learned the greatest lesson of her life before becoming a Multi-Millionaire.

Sissy made it her business to use *"The Guarded Psalms of Prayer"* to better herself, as she was not going to allow the mental and emotional abuse of her past to hinder her future. For that reason, she began to pray for her daily bread as she recited the scripture in Philippians 4:13, *"I can do all things through Christ which strengthens me."* As Sissy stepped into millionaire status, she has learned how to say, "NO" to those who choose to use her kindness as a weakness. In business, she now has over 1000 employees, while her sister Margaret is still stuck on the same level of doing business.

After all of her struggles, she wants us to learn how to trust God in all things regardless of our past abuses, hang-ups, and setbacks in life. Flaws are inevitable, we all have them. From time-to-time we will all feel as if nothing's working for us; however, if we allow our flaws to create undue pressure, then we will have a problem.

Luke 15:11-32 shows us how we can fall by the wayside so easily: Then He said: *"A certain man had two sons. And the younger of them said to his father, 'Father, give me the portion of goods that falls to me.' So he divided to them his livelihood. And not many days after, the younger son gathered all together, journeyed to a far country, and there wasted his possessions with prodigal living. But when he had spent all, there arose a severe famine in that land, and he began to be in want. Then he went and joined himself to a citizen of that country, and he sent him into his fields to feed swine. And he would gladly have filled his stomach with the pods that the swine ate, and no one gave him anything. But when he came to himself, he said, 'How many of my father's hired servants have bread enough and to spare, and I perish with hunger! I will arise and go to my father, and will say to him, "Father, I have sinned against heaven and before you, and I am no longer worthy to be called your son. Make me like one of your hired servants."' And he arose and came to his father. But when he was still a great way off, his father saw him and had compassion, and ran and fell on his neck and kissed him. And the son said to him, 'Father, I have sinned against heaven and in your sight, and am no longer worthy to be called your son.' But the father said to his servants, 'Bring out the best robe and put it on him, and put a ring on his hand and sandals on his feet. And bring the fatted calf here and kill it, and let us eat and be merry; for this my son was dead and is alive again; he was lost and is found.' And they began to be merry. Now his older son was in the field. And as he came and drew near to the house, he heard music and dancing. So he called one of the servants and asked what these things meant. And he said to him, 'Your brother has come, and*

Chapter 10 | Madam Oracle

because he has received him safe and sound, your father has killed the fatted calf.' But he was angry and would not go in. Therefore, his father came out and pleaded with him. So he answered and said to his father, 'Lo, these many years I have been serving you; I never transgressed your commandment at any time; and yet you never gave me a young goat, that I might make merry with my friends. But as soon as this son of yours came, who has devoured your livelihood with harlots, you killed the fatted calf for him.' And he said to him, 'Son, you are always with me, and all that I have is yours. It was right that we should make merry and be glad, for your brother was dead and is alive again, and was lost and is found.' "

Just remember that limitations of our flaws are created in the mind when there is codependency residing in the heart. Everything that we do, say, or react to, contributes to the way in which we deal with ourselves, as well as the way in which we deal with or help others. Challenges will come, and challenges will go; therefore, we must determine what we hold on to when the challenges leave. Some hold on to resentment, some hold on to anger, some hold on to fear and some hold on to the ability to let go. Regardless of what we hold on to, we are held accountable for what we do with and how we react to our experiences. You are here to make a difference! It is through you that a certain amount of people can be reached, and it's your responsibility to make a positive impact on them, regardless of your set of challenges.

When dealing with self, it's okay to use our expectations to solve a problem, make a change, or empower ourselves because we are not born confident—it is a character trait that is learned. Most often, we will find that confidence is confused with arrogance and vice-versa. Confidence displays the security and strength to take charge, to make changes as well as make effective decisions; whereas, arrogance is the opposite. We will find that arrogant people are really insecure, using the illusion of strength to cover up hidden weaknesses. I feel that whatever we have learned in the past can be unlearned, if we are willing to change our expectations and work through our weaknesses to free ourselves.

Prayer

Father my God, in the Name of Jesus, I take authority over all negative words spoken by me and others over my life. Not only that, I take authority over my thoughts, actions, reactions, and the governing of my state of mind. I bind all thoughts of negativity and defeat, as I loose myself from the wiles of the enemy on the outside, or on the inside of me. By the Blood of the Lamb, I come against all self-defeating or tormenting thoughts that have been harassing my state of mind. I curse and destroy the root of fears, doubts, worries, and anxieties that are causing me to become defeated in the area in which I should be excelling. Therefore, I rebuke the devourer of my positivity and I ask for forgiveness regarding my insensitivity toward having a positive mental attitude.

Father my God which art in Heaven, I relinquish my mind to You, I relinquish my thoughts to You, I relinquish my attitude to You, I relinquish my body to You, I relinquish my soul to You, and I relinquish my spirit to You. Without You, I am nothing—without You, I would truly fail; therefore, I give all of me to see through Your Eyes to ensure that I develop a positive outlook on life, Your way. In the Name of Jesus, I pray that You reveal to me all that ungodly or negative actions, reactions, behaviors, habits, thoughts, and beliefs that I am knowingly and unknowingly aware of— so that I can better understand the power of having a Christ-like positive mindset.

As of today, I will no longer become a victim of vain thoughts and imaginations that destroys my positive state of mind. For that reason, I will only speak blessing on myself and others. In Jesus' Name.

Scripture Reading:

Psalms 62
Psalms 76
Psalms 95
Psalms 105

CHAPTER 11

The Principle of Psalms

We cannot save everyone, but it's our responsibility to do our part in making a true difference. Throughout my journey in life, I have found that communication is one of our most invaluable commodities. If we have a desire to be understood, we must first understand through effective listening. When we do not listen, we will find that we tend to miss out on the essence of what true living is all about.

This story really moved me: *"While in the heart of beautiful downtown Orlando, a man sat down next to a woman on a bench near the swan rides at Lake Eola Park. "That's my daughter over there," he said, pointing to a cute little red-head girl who was mesmerized by the beautiful swans that were walking around freely without a care in the world. "She's a cutie pie, and* that's my son on the swan boat ride," the woman said. Then, looking at her watch, she called to her son. *"It's time to go, Blake."* Blake pleaded, *"Just one more ride, Mom. Please....Just one more ride, please."* The woman nodded, and Blake continued another 30-minute ride. When the ride ended, she said: *"Let's go, Blake, we need to leave, we have already spent $36.00 on this Swan ride."* Again Blake pleaded, *"One more time, Mom. Just one more."* The woman politely smiled and said, *"OK, we only have enough money for one more ride."* The man next to her said, *"My, you do not see too many mothers as patient as you are."* The woman smiled and then said, *"I waited 20 years for God to bless me with a son; therefore, the time that his dad and I spend with him is well worth understanding his need to have fun. My goal is to listen and understand his wants, needs, and desires, so if Blake needs 30 more minutes to ride on the Swan, that means that I have 30 more minutes to understand that he is worth the time that I spend waiting on him."*

This woman took the time to digest "The Guarded Psalms of Prayer" in order to exercise patience and the value of spending quality time with her son.

When we are at the crossroad of survival, the thoughts that we think determines the real essence of who we are, what we will become, what or whom we attract and which direction we take. One of the biggest issues that we all face is to figure out what to do with our lives. Nevertheless, in the figuring process, we often get our insurance policies together preparing for death, forgetting about preparing to live. Living our lives to the

Chapter 11 | Madam Oracle

fullest is often overlooked because we become so busy going from here to there—not realizing that there is more to life than our present situation.

I ran across this story several years ago, *"One day a farmer's donkey fell down into a well. The helpless donkey cried pitifully for hours as the little old farmer tried to figure out what he was going to do. Finally, he decided the animal was old, he has already gotten the use out of him and the well needed to be covered up anyway—it just was not worth it to rescue the donkey from the well. So he decided that he would invite all of his neighbors over to help him cover up the poor old donkey. They all grabbed a shovel and began to scoop dirt into the well. When the donkey realized that his master gave up on him, he cried. He could not believe that he served his master for so many years, and now that he is in a predicament, his master gave up on him without a fight. Then, to the amazement of everyone, he stopped crying. He decided to do something about his situation. The more they piled dirt on him, the more he used it as a stepping stone to get out of his predicament. As the farmer and his friends kept shoveling dirt, they finally looked down and saw that the donkey was not settling for defeat. Every time they shovel dirt on the donkey, he would shake it off and take another step up—the farmer and his friends could not believe the donkey was smart enough to step up out of his situation. Soon enough, the donkey stepped right over the edge and walked off, leaving his old master behind."*

Our enemies will become our footstool of greatness if we allow him or her to play his or her role in our lives without becoming bitter about the circumstances or situation that's presented to us. It's through our enemies that we will find our *"Mind of Mastery"* and understanding if we do not become emotional. Our emotions inhibit our ability to grab the source of wisdom needed to make all of our enemies become the footstool that's propelling us to the next level; therefore, it's imperative that we allow our enemies to make us better and not bitter. When we are bitter, we actually prevent wisdom from attaching itself to us; as a matter of fact, bitterness opens the door to jealousy and envy, to further break down the emotional bond; therefore, breaking down the relationship.

It does not matter what people think or say about you that matters, it's what you are saying about you that really makes the difference. So what if people throw dirt at you or on you—just step up to the next level with your head up high as you learn how to develop the voice within, the counselor of your higher self. God, has given you the Holy Spirit as your counselor; why not allow Him to work for you and through you to accomplish your goals and aspirations in life.

Prayer

Father my God, which art in Heaven, I lift up my hands to You, in the Mighty Name of Jesus. I am seeking confidence from You to become held in high esteem with myself, and others. You have overcome the World with a confidence beyond human comprehension, and being that I am created in Your image, that same confidence resides within me as well. Therefore, by divine decree, I invoke the supernatural confidence that can only come from You, because we are one in Christ Jesus. From this day forward, I am entering the most Holy Place, and that is into Your presence, seeking the courage and the strength to move beyond my self-imposed limitations.

Given the price Jesus paid on the Cross for me, I know beyond a shadow of a doubt that You will not withhold any good thing; therefore, I humbly plead that You bring forth the high esteem that's buried deep within the depths of my soul. For that reason O' Lord, I am now calling the Deep unto the Deep, reaching into the inner treasures of the greater unknown to bring forth that in which I am destined to do, say, and become. I will no longer wallow in the shadows of low esteem, defeat, or insecurity, because greater is in me, than he that's in the world.

As a Child of the Most High, I now lay claim to the GREATER from within, while releasing the superficial facades of what others think of me. You know the issues of my heart, and it is only You that can truly heal them with no strings attached. For that reason, I am digging deep to bring forth the seeds of greatness that will not fall by the wayside, among the thorns, or under a rock, but on fertile ground that will bring forth after its own kind, putting away the secrets of being that in which I am not.

As I draw near to You, cleanse and forgive me of anything that is not of You; therefore, giving me a clear conscience to become one with the Body of Christ. On this day, I am rising up to confidently walk in high esteem as my faith makes me whole, with no regrets attached to it. For this high esteem, O' Lord, I give thanks to You, while Your praises continually flow from my lips. Amen.

<u>Scripture Reading:</u>

Psalms 23
Psalms 25
Psalms 40
Psalms 65
Psalms 66

CHAPTER 12
Simple Life with Psalms

We sometimes suffer in a good way, and sometimes we suffer in a bad way; however, we do not have to become bound by our suffering, because we have the Tree of Life left. After that one act of disobedience from Adam & Eve in the Garden of Eden, God has hidden the Tree of Life in plain sight, which means that if we are not ready to see it (the solution), we will not see it, no matter how hard we try! Why do we have to pay for the sins of Adam and Eve? It is not a matter of paying for the sins of another; it's a matter of living through the sins of our forefathers.

Although we are blessed, the afflictions of life have enough power to make us doubt what we actually believe—so much so that we wallow in self-pity, as we begin to stop loving ourselves. Of course, it has happened to the best of us, and if this has not happened at some point in our lives, just live a little longer—life does have a way of squeezing us until we break or produce, love or hate, succeed or fail, win or lose, etc. In my opinion, we cannot get the oil out of the olive unless we squeeze it; or better yet, we cannot enjoy orange juice, if the orange is not squeezed. Most often, our blessing will not reveal itself until we are squeezed, tried, rooted, grounded, and tested.

Love has its own language; it has its own agenda; it has its own uniqueness that will capture the heart of those who learn how to use it gracefully. What we most often do not realize is that love is also a responsibility for each and every one of us. Although there is a big difference between loving people and being in love with a person, but we must also understand that we are all accountable for living life or feeling alive while living. I feel very strongly that our level of LOVE differentiates the two, but we as individuals must choose our own path to find out what or who works for us and what or who does not.

We often hear that *"Iron Sharpens Iron"* Proverbs 27:17. *"The Guarded Psalms of Prayer"* believes that wholeheartedly; however, it is also true that *"Iron sharpens love"* as well. The more we use it positively, the stronger it becomes. However, the more we abuse it negatively, the more it cuts to the core, creating sore spots that may cause one to become overly sensitive, too emotional,

Chapter 12 | Madam Oracle

uncontrollable, or mentally unstable. Therefore, we must learn how to use love, when to use it, where to use it, and why we should use it, to prevent love from cutting us in places that we should not be cut, cutting us in places that we should have healed, or wounding innocent people.

Love is not about being weak; it's about being humble. Yes, humility will take us places where a stone-cold heart can never keep us. This does not mean that one cannot exhibit tough love, it means that one can humbly love and exhibit positive strength at the same time. There is nothing weak about this type of individual—they are very polite, confident, knows what they want, and do not have to abuse love to get it. Plus, in Ephesians 5:25, *"Husbands are commanded to love their wives as Christ loves the church."* Trust that when this truly happens, they will become incomplete without each other; not in a codependent way, but in an interdependent way as a team—where one is weak, the other one is strong and vice versa. Of course, no one is perfect; we are all a work in progress, but it is our attitude and behaviors that reveal the true testament of our love in any relationship without us having to say one word. Here are the subtle, but effective signs of love that I look for in a relationship: submissiveness, attentiveness, respectfulness, gentleness, and helpfulness.

Affection is designed for everyone, and we all desire it, even if we pretend as if we do not. Make no mistake about it, we all have a little kid inside of us, regardless of whether we are all grown up or not. We just need to feel safe when allowing that little kid out to play. If we hide our inner child, we will tend to become a little uptight about life, and we will tend to lose our enjoyment for it as well. Soon thereafter, it becomes harder and harder for us to laugh and truly enjoy ourselves....when the Bible clearly states that *"Laughter is Medicine for the Soul"* Proverbs 17:22. Personally, I cannot imagine living life without laughing a lot—it truly brings joy to my heart. However, I know when to laugh and when to take life seriously as well—I guess, this is where balance comes into play, but it does not impede upon my ability to remain affectionate at all times.

Truly affectionate people know how to express love to those who are open and willing to receive it with no strings attached. Affection is not sexuality or sensuality at all; it is being able to exhibit kindness in a physical form through our actions, gestures, and words to provoke the feelings or emotions of someone. Now, on the other hand, if someone is using affection with strings attached, I would consider that a form of control, manipulation, or conditional affection, which is often used when playing with someone's emotions or playing the game of love. This type of affection can become dangerous, especially when a person feels as if they are being duped. I do not advise this sort of behavior because innocent people can get hurt—if one does not have a desire to be with someone, make it clear up-front!

Although, everyone is not open to every form of affection; however, we are able to fill them out to see what works best. Everyone is different in their own unique or subtle way—there is no need to become overbearing with affection; in my opinion, it's the little things in life that have the most profound impact. I would call this proactive thinking—thinking about the needs of an individual before the need presents itself. For example, if the lawn guy is cutting the grass, why not take him a bottle of water before he gets thirsty. In so many words, do not wait for him to get thirsty, provide the resources to quench the thirst before he gets thirsty. This is a nice gesture that exhibits friendly affection and Godly character without any ulterior motive.

"The Guarded Psalms of Prayer" ways to Sharpen Love:

- Greet people
- Smile often
- Make eye contact when speaking to someone
- Verbalize appreciation or love
- Give gifts of appreciation or love
- Proactively think about an individual's needs
- Pay attention to the moods and offer positive encouragement
- An appropriate subtle, natural touch
- A kiss, hug, or tickle works well

- Holding someone when appropriate
- Surprises are great
- Notes are awesome
- Eat together
- Pray together
- Never appear busy, even if you are. Patience is GOLDEN
- Set aside time for a person, place, or thing
- Communicate often
- Play or have fun often
- Do not be afraid to grab someone's hand
- Sincerely ask about a person's well-being
- Look for ways to be a blessing
- Always hopeful
- Warm and sincere with others

"The Guarded Psalms of Prayer" list of items that cause our love to become dull or repulsive:

- Nagging
- Whining
- Criticizing self and others
- Indecisiveness or always wishy-washy
- Negative
- Fake and abrasive
- Cannot accept responsibility

- Intentionally hurting others
- Yelling
- Fighting
- Addicted to chaos
- Always giving ultimatums
- Putting people in a box
- Lack the initiative to become proactive
- Hateful
- Rude
- Lying
- Abrasive
- Arrogant
- Disobedient
- Disrespectful
- Unhelpful
- Kicking people when they are down
- Expecting more than we are willing to give
- Contentious

When we exhibit dull and repulsive behaviors, we will find that life will pull us into an unpleasant place mentally, emotionally, physically, and spiritually. A dry, dull place or drought in life is a time of self-correction. *"The Guarded Psalms of Prayer"* says that a drought is nature's way of correcting itself to keep universal balance and harmony. This principle is applicable to every aspect of life; therefore, a drought does not enter our lives to kill us—it comes to heal us in places that we are knowingly or unknowingly wounded, handicapped, or disobedient.

Of course, we are all a work in progress; however, when we stop progressing in the area of our purpose or when we become codependent, we will find that we will begin to thirst for something or someone that's not conducive to our well-being. When we quench our thirst with the wrong thing, it will keep us all over the place mentally and emotionally, it will keep us running to and fro in our busyness accomplishing nothing, or it will keep us wallowing in a bed of indecisiveness that will delay our bountiful harvest that's most often noticeable in our ability to love effectively. *"The Guarded Psalms of Prayer"* encourage you to take the time to master those dry or thirsty places in your life to ensure that you do not defy the purpose of your drought or your reason for loving God, yourself, and others.

Making Sense

We all try to understand and make sense of life when it may not be for us to understand. The bigger issue is taking what you have, whether you understand it or not, and placing it into the hands of God, instead of forcing people, places, and things where they do not belong. Let Him work those things that are beyond your human comprehension out. One of my favorite scriptures regarding this is located in Isaiah 5:8 *"For my thoughts are not your thoughts, neither are your ways my ways.*" "*The Guarded Psalms of Prayer*" says that this is God's way of letting us know that thinking is a reliable asset to pursue our destiny. But, overthinking could be a hindrance to us, especially when we out think the essence of true wisdom and obedience.

"*The Guarded Psalms of Prayer*" also says that panicking over life is not going to change anything, nor will it help us with our belief system; it will only create more stress than necessary. Listed below are a few things that will help your belief system:

1. KNOW YOUR PURPOSE!
2. Know that everything works for your good.
3. You are responsible for you.
4. Remain teachable!
5. You cannot blame anyone for your mishaps.
6. Assume responsibility for your life.
7. Use your shortcomings as hidden strengths.
8. Look for the good in everything.
9. Finish what you start.
10. Take a "time-out" for yourself.
11. Pray and Meditate every day.
12. Never lose your sense of humor and smile.
13. Face your problems and never deny that they exist.
14. Give yourself positive affirmations.
15. Commit to working on the undeveloped areas of your life.

16. Know that you are the best at what you do.
17. Do everything in the spirit of excellence.
18. Accept rejection without allowing your ego to become bruised.
19. If you fall, get back up again.
20. Refuse to have a pity party.
21. Refuse to be a victim—you are a victor!
22. Steer clear of toxic people.
23. Never complicate things, keep life simple.
24. Make sure everything is in writing; write out your visions, goals, etc.
25. Keep track of your blessings.
26. Read every day.
27. Spend time on your goal(s) 6 out of 7 days a week.

As we develop our *"Mind of Mastery,"* we must ensure that everyone feels superior or worthy; regardless of whether we feel as if it's deserved or not. It is our responsibility to treat others the way we want to be treated. Rest assured that if we provoke fear or insecurity in others, we will find that we bring those same attributes back to our own house. If we want to bring blessings to our house—our best bet is to motivate, encourage and inspire others.

We as a people must recognize that we are a source of inspiration to someone, and it is through that disappointment that we unawaringly lead those who look up to us astray. Nevertheless, it is our responsibility as a child of the Most High to lead without intentionally causing dismay to those who are counting on us to lead them. Every generation must become better than the previous one, and if we are digressing in that formality, we must gain control over our lives to leave a legacy worth leaving behind. We have not gone through all of our challenges for nothing; we have not overcome insurmountable defeat to allow it to go in vain—it is time to gird up our loins, get back on track, and live the life that God has predestined for us to live. Everything we need is already within us, every experience has provided a roadmap for us to follow, and all we need to do is become a master over our mind, instincts, emotions, exercise love, and utilize our divine wisdom from within.

Although we may not be able to explain a lot of things about our lives, what's taking place, or the reasons why. But if we can embrace or open ourselves up to the Wisdom of God, I promise that He will redefine everything about our mind, our emotions, our instincts, and our ability to love; therefore, giving us the ability to move into our faith and favor at the appropriate time. Let me say this, faith and favor without God will render one's mind scattered, emotions all over the place, and our instincts ineffective. In my opinion, if that is what's happening, it is better to use the tool that God has given us to gain our POWER back, and that is the power of PRAYER.

"The Guarded Psalms of Prayer" wants you to know that all you have to do is stop trying to overcomplicate life, learn to live in peace, pray about everything, love effectively, and embrace the Wisdom of God to govern your mind, your emotions, and your instincts. Once this is done, I promise you that the Mind, Body, Soul, and Spirit will make a true believer out of you, changing your whole outlook on life!

When we have an imbalance in our perspectives, we will find that we will become a little wishy-washy, not knowing what we want in life or who we are. However, if we dare to take time out to pay attention to *"The Guarded Psalms of Prayer,"* we will find that we are better able to fit in or balance a relationship, even if we are dealing with a really difficult individual. In my opinion, difficult people are not really difficult, they are just misunderstood—they simply overcompensate in their behavior to be heard by someone who truly understands his or her perspective in life.

Prayer

My God, in the mighty Name of Jesus, I am asking that You build my faith in my known, and unknown areas of weakness. I know that when I am weak, then I am strong; and, that my faith is indeed the substance of things hoped for, and the evidence of things that I cannot see. Therefore, I give my instincts to You, as You build my faith from the ground up, instilling that

24-hour faith in me. Plus, as a faithful and humble servant, I am convinced that if my instincts become Yours, then we are one in Christ Jesus.

As the Author and Finisher of my faith, I believe that my instincts, along with my faith will serve You, and Your righteousness all day long, while Your precepts permeate into the depths of my heart. Therefore, granting me wisdom beyond all human understanding, as You keep my feet from straying away from the path You have rightfully designed for me. My God, in the name of Jesus, with all that being said, one thing I know is that my faith and hope goes hand-in-hand, as I embark upon this moment-by-moment walk with You. Furthermore, as the cycle of life continues, I also know that as long as I have life flowing through my body, I will always have hope, and something to believe in. For that reason, on this day, I pray that You grant me the strength to hold on; and, to keep my head up even when it doesn't seem as if things are in my favor.

Lord, in Your everlasting grace and mercy, Your Word has become my weapon of warfare, a lamp under my feet, and a light unto my path; therefore, enhancing my ability to worship and praise You from the depths of my very own soul. For that reason, I pray for the confidence, and courage needed to enable me to walk by faith and not by sight. Father, in the mighty Name of Jesus, I also pray that You grant me the wisdom, the understanding, and the instincts to move at the right time, or to hold my peace, while You are working things out in my favor to build my faith regarding the people, places, and things that I've hoped for. With that being said, You are my refuge and my strength; let nothing come in between my instinctual faith that has been designed to take me to the next level. For this, O' Lord, I give thanks to You and Your praises will be continually on my lips. Amen.

Scripture Reading:

Psalms 27
Psalms 39
Psalms 57
Psalms 71
Psalms 119
Psalms 122

CHAPTER 13

True Gift of Psalms

"The Guarded Psalms of Prayer" says that we need people, and people need us. I know that there is a lot of hype about being independent; and, yes, we all should be independent assuming responsibility for our own life. However, we must also have an openness to interdependency as well. Interdependency is our ability to work together with people to accomplish a common goal in the "WE" form—in so many words, "Teamwork."

People will tell you how they want to be treated, and they will also tell you why. They know what they are looking for better than anyone else, and all we have to do is "Break the ice." This can be done by asking fact-finding questions, and repeating back to them what you have heard. This will tell them that you were paying attention to them. It is through our rationalizing and justification that cause us to make costly mistakes; therefore, wasting valuable time pursuing someone who's going to elude us anyway. This can be avoided if we just listen to them—listen to what they are saying, what they are not saying, listen to their body language, and listen to LIFE. Life has a way of telling you things that people are afraid to tell you; but, you must hone into LISTENING very well.

Our interconnectedness and interdependency with others is a great way to achieve that in which we cannot do for ourselves. There are times when greater success can be attained through a combined effort of those who are able to accentuate the greatness that's already within us, without us becoming dependent upon them. Of course, trust must be developed in some way; however, it should never prevent us from becoming a team player in all that we do, say, or think. In order to maximize our interdependency, we must hone into our ability to become a motivator or motivatee. As we all know, motivation is the key factor in communicating effectively with self, others, and our environment.

Our environment has a paramount effect on us whether we admit it or not. If our environment is comprised of selfishness—we have a tendency to become selfish as well, if we do not take the initiative to make the necessary changes. When we become willing to exhaust all of our resources, we therefore, put ourselves in a position to overcome any known or unknown adversity that prevents us from taking responsibility for ourselves. Once this is accomplished, *"The Guarded Psalms of Prayer"* says that it will give us the ability to achieve the desires of our heart or give us the R.O.A.R.ing courage to get rid of what's not working in our environment. We are the paradigm of our environment, we are the paradigm of our belief system, we are the paradigm of our thoughts, we are the paradigm of our actions, and we are the paradigm of our attitude. If we want our paradigm to change, we must change or adjust our level of dependency and responsibility of our mindset.

It is through your mindset that governs your beliefs, and it is through your beliefs that govern the perception you have over your reality or the perspective that you have about yourself. My friend, it's imperative that you avail yourself to become interconnected with your environment; therefore, enabling you to better understand whether the people, places, and things in your life are enhancing or limiting your full potential.

Now let me ask you this: Is your cup half full, or is your cup half-empty? I have been asked this question time without number, and my answer has always remained the same. I am not settling for my cup to be half-full or half empty when I am indeed the cup. I take ownership, so it doesn't matter whether my cup is half-full, half empty, completely full, or completely empty, "I am IT!" We are conditioned to always say that our cup is half-full, so why can we not be conditioned to take ownership of our lives? Passing the buck just to be accepted or to eliminate the feeling of rejection is unacceptable. We must learn how to OWN IT, whatever our "IT" is, regardless if it's right, wrong, or indifferent. If we own it, we can refill it at any given moment or we can allow it to run over....WE CHOOSE.

10 WAYS TO PROTECT YOUR GIFT

1. Value your privacy. People will deplete you of all your energy if you allow them to.
2. Guard your thoughts. Your thoughts create your reality.
3. Focus on the wants and not the DO NOT WANTS.
4. Be cautious about where you get your information.
5. Exercise caution regarding who you allow into your life.
6. Know that your potential can cause the actual.
7. Consider yourself blessed at all times.
8. Never be afraid to say goodbye to the past and hello to your future.
9. Understand that you have been chosen for your own unique assignment.
10. Plan your life to create a wall of success.

"*The Guarded Psalms of Prayer*" says that we are not the Lone Ranger in this wonderful thing called Life. If a person needs help, give it! If someone genuinely offers to help, take it! If we need to delegate, delegate. Outsourcing is a great way to delegate things to maintain balance in our lives. There is no need to impress others with what we are, what we do, what we own, what we say, or what we want to become. It's okay to be who we are as long as we understand that our gift will make room for us. In so many words, when we trust and believe in who we are, what we have, or want to become—everything in our lives will begin to position itself to bless us, if we maximize the Power of Forgiveness.

Gift of Forgiveness

When we hit the RESET button on our emotions making a choice to forgive, we are better able to glean from the vestibule of grace and mercy when it's our turn to be forgiven. It is not a matter of IF we need forgiveness; it's a matter of WHEN. We are all a work in progress, regardless of how well we paint the picture; therefore, we must exercise our God-given right to forgive to ensure that when we fall short, grace and mercy becomes a shield to cover us even when we cannot foresee the wiles of the enemy. I am not saying that we will not get angry, but *"Be angry, yet do not sin. Do not let the sun set while you are still angry,"* according to Ephesians 4:26.

If we need to vent, go ahead and do so; but, by the time the sun sets in the west, so should our anger. And, make sure forgiveness resides in our heart before we go to bed to ensure that we are able to have peace while we are sleeping. Unforgiveness is the main contributor to what we call insomnia; therefore, we must cleanse our soul of this negative emotion as soon as possible. Do I have my moments? Absolutely! There are times when I just want to stay mad, especially when my kindness is taken as a weakness. But, I have trained myself so well until I cannot stay mad for long, even if I tried. I will forget about being mad, because my mind will automatically move on to a happy state of being, superseding my emotions.

"The Guarded Psalms of Prayer" says that once the Spirit of Forgiveness becomes a part of who we are, grudges are less likely to be held against someone. Unless there is a severe psychological trauma that may have occurred that would cause that individual to temporary harbor unforgiveness. However, in order to move beyond any type of trauma, forgiveness must take place whether it's a part of our character or not. It's okay to hit that reset button on your emotions, on your forgiveness, or your favor, it is a gift that can be utilized at any given moment. Today, forgive yourself and forgive those who have trespassed against you to ensure that you are able to be forgiven in your moment of need.

Gift of Pronoia

How do we triumph over a setback? *"The Guarded Psalms of Prayer"* says that overcoming a setback has to become a mindset; if not, one will continue to live that setback over and over again without doing anything about it. In my opinion, setbacks are hidden lessons to bring us into the classroom of life.

The pronoia effect is profound, and it works like a charm! Pronoia is basically getting our mind into thinking that everyone is here to help us out, teach us a lesson that we have been overlooking, or guide us in some way. Once we understand that everyone enters our life for a reason, for a season, or for a lifetime, we are better able to move on in the Spirit of Love without holding any sort of resentment. And, if we do not understand what God is trying to say to us, what God is trying to teach us, what direction God is trying to lead us in, what corrections that we need to make in our lives, or what has become god in our lives over Him, that lesson will continue to repeat itself until we get it. Therefore, there is no reason to blame anyone for our setbacks—it's never about them, it's always about us. We have to look from within to find the lesson, and once we find the lesson, it is wrapped in Divine Wisdom.

Listen to me, this is how I view the pronoia effect in my life: a setback for me is wisdom being handed to me on a silver platter—I eat it up, and I share it to activate the Law of Reciprocity. When I am served a setback, obstacle, or difficult situation, I become a student, learning the lesson from it; and then, I turn around to become the teacher to empower others to open the floodgate of wisdom. Seed, time, and harvest apply to our setbacks as well; and it cannot hold us back if we simply set it up to become a blessing for ourselves and others. If we can find a way to learn from our setbacks and create a win-win situation by looking for the positive without focusing on the negative, wisdom will be waiting to provide us with the substance or provisions needed to overcome the situation, circumstance, or event.

"The Guarded Psalms of Prayer" says that a setback is a distraction to keep us blind, confused, and frustrated with ourselves. However, when we exercise wisdom, compassion, love, and due diligence when dealing with a setback, we are better able to maneuver around obstacles to achieve our desired goals. Here is a prime example, if we crush an ant mound, we will never see them weeping, becoming depressed, or settling for defeat. We will see them scurry for safety; and, they will rebuild that mound by any means necessary; regardless of whether we want them there or not. It is sad to say, but it is only death that will stop an ant from rebuilding its empire. And, the same should apply to us—it does not matter what people think about us or our situation; we must keep ourselves busy building, without weeping over people, places, and things that we cannot change or have control over.

If something or someone rains on our parade, simply dry off, regroup, get a strategy, and go for it again! A true winner will not stop because of a setback; they simply learn from it, and find another way. If you take nothing else from this book, please take heed to this: leave no stone unturned; regardless of how it may appear. *"The Guarded Psalms of Prayer"* says that your blessings will never appear as such....your best bet is to refrain from settling for defeat mentally, do what you have to do to overcome your setbacks emotionally, and keep yourself moving physically, to ensure that you do not have any regrets about giving up on YOU. Oh by the way, if you add a little prayer to it, you will indeed enhance your Spiritual Powerhouse causing the spirit of defeat to flee. Yes, prayer is like the icing on the cake that bridges the triumphant gap commencing all things to work together for your good.

Prayer

Success, Success, come to me now—Success, Success, you know how. My Father which art in Heaven, in the Mighty Name of Jesus, I invoke the success of my inner man to come forth right now. My God, for the weapons of warfare are not carnal, but for the pulling down of strongholds that are keeping me from excelling into greatness; therefore, I put my trust in You, O' Lord. You are my Rock and my Salvation, whom shall I fear—for I know that You will not withhold any good thing from me, nor will any good opportunities pass over me.

Lord, I stand on Your word that my Gift will make room for me, and set me before men in high places.

And, for that reason, in the Name of Jesus, I pray that You sharpen my instincts to know what's right for me, and what's wrong for me, while I am on this journey into success. I know that trials and tests will come, but I am asking that You prepare me in advance for the woes of life, to ensure that I am strong and wise enough to handle what comes my way.

Father, as I attract success into my life, I am asking that You become the lamp under my feet, and the light unto my path as I walk by faith, and not by sight. For, Lord, You are my help in the time of my present need; and, without You, I cannot fully attain what destiny has for me. Therefore, from this day forward, I am pulling my strength from the Lion of Judah, as I bow down to You, my Heavenly Father, the King of Glory. Today, I come before You with clean hands and a pure heart seeking Your wisdom on how to succeed in all that I do, say, and become.

As a Child of the Most High, You said, if I seek, I will find. You also said, if I knock, the door shall be opened. For that reason, I am seeking and knocking for Your Divine Order, to bring forth that in which belongs to me, with no sorrow attached to it. Father, as I live with the mental concept of "**NO REGRETS**," let me not be put to shame for the pursuit of the Greatness that You have place within the depths of my soul. Let not my enemies reign over me, but allow them to become my footstool, as You teach me Your will and Your way to

Divine Greatness, in the Name of Jesus. Thank You. Amen.

Scripture Reading:
Psalms 5
Psalms 19
Psalms 26
Psalms 75
Psalms 122

CHAPTER 14

Psalms of Love

Even though people did not like me, they could not STOP me from my purpose. LOVE kept me safe. LOVE kept me humble. LOVE kept me protected. LOVE forgave me. LOVE disciplined me. LOVE empowered me. LOVE gave me mercy. LOVE gave me favor. LOVE gave me wisdom. LOVE blessed me. And, most of all, it was LOVE that granted me FREEDOM. The SECRET is that the outsider's love is indeed the love I give outside of myself. Hate cannot give me the promises of God. Hate cannot help me to reach into the depths of your soul. Hate cannot take me into places where I desire for God to keep me. Hate cannot give me the freedom that I so desire. *"The Guarded Psalms of Prayer"* says that it is LOVE that keeps the hate out of me; and, it is Love that will keep the hate out of you.

How do we deal with people who do not like us? If someone does not like us, that is their problem, not ours, unless we have given them a reason to dislike us. If someone does not get to know the true person that we are, then it's time to move on anyway. If we are doing the right thing by operating in outright integrity, we do not need to convince a person to like us, nor do we have to change who we are to fit into a particular circle just to become likable. It is imperative that we come into our own individuality; as long as we are not operating in waywardness to cause people to dislike us, then we have nothing to worry about. In my opinion, it is only envy, jealousy, or hatefulness that would cause one to dislike those who they know nothing about.

If we are exhibiting negative characteristics to offend, betray, or hurt innocent people, then one should have the option to dislike our behavior, attitude, action, or reaction. It does not matter what we do, say, or become, someone is not going to like it, or someone may have something to say about it; but we cannot allow it to stop us from becoming who God created us to be. Our value does not reside in someone liking us; our value resides in us liking ourselves for who we are.

"The Guarded Psalms of Prayer" says that when we lose value in ourselves, we will depend on others to value us instead; and, when that does not happen, we will feel as if we are unworthy of his or her love. In my opinion,

that should not be the case, but it happens all too often. How do we know if we are valuable to someone? We will know if someone values us when we find value in ourselves first. If we do not find value in ourselves, we will not appreciate the fact that a person has found us to be valuable; therefore, we will become ungrateful, taking more than we are giving. This is exactly how people tend to get used and abused because most often people will treat us based on how we see and treat ourselves, unless they are being vindictive trying to break down a person who takes pride in themselves. Nevertheless, we can spot those types of individuals by where they place their value; as a rule of thumb, what we find value in gets our love, time, money, priority, and other resources. If we pay closer attention to this, it will indeed safeguard one from a lot of deceptive people.

What we value enables us to set priorities of what's important to us; but when our values are not in the right place, we will find that we will begin to make bad decisions, wrong decisions, or controlling decisions based upon where our heart is. Listen, where there is no value found in what we have to offer, we must find a way to get into an environment where our true value is found. In so many words, deal with people that bring out the best and not the worst—when we become better, and not bitter about how we live our lives, as well as how we see ourselves, our whole outlook on life will change.

Knowing your values enable you to set priorities of what's important to you; it will also help you get rid of the people, places, and things that are not conducive to where you are going as well. You deserve the best, so operate in integrity doing everything in the Spirit of Excellence, and watch how the doors of blessings swing wide-open for you.

Looking Back

As we look back over our lives, where we are now, is a byproduct of the choices that we have made, and nothing will change unless we do. As long as the earth rotates on its axis, people will see us three ways: 1. They will see us how we see ourselves. 2. They will see us how they see themselves. 3. They will see the truth about who we are without being biased in their perception. Now, what really matters is how we see ourselves! *"The Guarded Psalms of Prayer"* says that until we understand and acknowledge the truth about who we are and why we are here, we will become aloof when people express how they feel or what they think about us; therefore, contributing to our bad attitude or our antisocialism. We are who we are, and there is nothing wrong with fine-tuning our ability to have a pleasant experience when we come in contact with others, or for others to have a pleasant experience in our presence.

The truth is that we are in control of who we are, and that should be our main focus. Regardless of what others think, do, or say, it is our responsibility to make a positive impact in our lives and in the lives of others. *"The Guarded Psalms of Prayer"* says that a simple smile, a word of encouragement, a helping hand, or a thank-you with a little love will make all the difference in the world. If we look around us, crimes are committed out of the lack of love in some area; suicides are committed out of the lack of love in some area; injustices are committed out of the lack of love in some area, and ill-wills are committed out of the lack of love in some area. All of these actions are directly linked to the inferiority complex that is also derived from the lack of love in some area as well. Can we get away from love? Absolutely not, LOVE is the common denominator in our actions, reactions, or the lack thereof. Believe it or not, we can find most of our answers to our failures, atrocities, or mishaps in life, if we simply narrow down the love or the lack of love associated with the situation, circumstance, or event that has caused us some sort of hiccup or discomfort in our lives.

When we lack compassion in a particular area, it is fair to say that there is some form of love deficit taking place. Although we may not look at it that way; however, if we really ask ourselves fact-finding questions regarding our behaviors, we will find that they are indeed linked back to LOVE in some way, shape, or form. *"The Guarded Psalms of Prayer"* is designed to have one to look at love from a different perspective, which is what I consider to be putting a "New Spin" on things. Some would say there is a right way to love, and one would say that there is a wrong way. *"The Guarded Psalms of Prayer"* says that Integral Love produces the foundation that helps us to love in spite of our differences, to help others without expecting anything in return, and to respect others with Universal Love.

We all hear about One Love, but what we do not hear about is Loving One.....A New Spin, right? Absolutely.....that's what I do.....I am here to get our minds to thinking a little bit. Who is the Loving One? If each one of us loves one, is that enough love to go around? If we love more than we hate, would we not have enough love to supply every human being on the face of this earth? Now, let's get back to the Loving One....are you the Loving One? Or, are you the Hateful One? There is no in-between on this; you can only be one or the other....from this point on....YOU CHOOSE! Hopefully, one would choose to become the Loving One, but let me say this, we are all a work in progress.

Our lovability may not happen overnight, but with our willingness to take a step to love one person at a time speaks volumes as we close the door on our hatefulness. *"The Guarded Psalms of Prayer"* says that hateful people do not realize that they are hateful, they do not realize that they are doing hateful things, and they do not realize that they are hurting others. As long as they are getting what they want, their conscience takes a back seat on their ability to love others who provide them with little or no benefits. There are a lot of

Chapter 14 | Madam Oracle

negative characteristics associated with hatefulness, and if one has a desire to maximize *"The Guarded Psalms of Prayer,"* they must lay aside hatefulness and the behaviors that are associated with this negative characteristic. Now, in order to do so, we must incorporate one of my BIG SECRETS! That SECRET is COMPASSION. We must include compassion into everything that we do, say, and become—this will overrule our hatefulness. Trust me, when it comes down to hatefulness vs. compassion—one or the other will rule! If one chooses compassion, it does not make us weak; it makes us WISE!

What is compassion? We can say that compassion is a lot of things; but in my opinion, it's real simple—our answer has always been in plain sight. COM-PASSION, COME PASSION = The Oracle-ism is to Come With Passion! When we exercise our God-given ability to approach everyone and every situation with passion (a serious desire, concern, sympathy, understanding, and respect for others), we put our hatefulness at bay. This is one characteristic that allows us to take SELF out of the way to genuinely help others without expecting anything in return.

Compassion is also one characteristic that will help us deal with our selfish behaviors; therefore, motivating us to go out of our way to do good deeds for those who are in need of our help or those who are in need of what we have to offer. It is imperative that we understand that we cannot expect compassion from others, but it must become a driving force from within the depths of our souls to exhibit compassion, regardless of how others treat us. I am not saying to become a doormat; what I am saying is that we do not have to become hateful just because people are hateful. *"The Guarded Psalms of Prayer"* says that the *"Tit For Tat"* hatefulness is a good remedy for getting hurt. If for some reason we are faced with this issue, it is always best to simply gird up our loins of compassion and walk away with our dignity intact. This rule applies to all types of relationships—fighting hatefulness with hatefulness is a recipe for disaster. And, regardless of how strong or trifling we think we are, we are all human! Just keep in mind that emotional, mental, or spiritual wounds or traumas may not show up for years!

The Goal of Love is to build lives, one at a time. But without compassion for the lives of others, it's hard to build and easier to destroy lives by default. If the truth is told, we have professional life builders, and we have professional life destroyers—the difference between the two are their level of compassion. Although most of us do not think much about our level of compassion; however, the real meaning of our purpose in life is encapsulated it.

"The Guarded Psalms of Prayer" says that we are all created to solve some sort of problem. If we are not able to offer compassion to others, it is a possibility that our purpose could be withheld until we are able to exhibit Godly characteristics; which are the true

foundation of living a fulfilled life. Trust me, it's enough to be broke and have a sad, empty life; but it's even worse to have a loaded bank account, and the money that we have cannot fill our emptiness or buy our happiness. Material gain, recognition, success, and big egos are not required for us to receive all that God has for us. *"The Guarded Psalms of Prayer"* says all we need is a willingness to LOVE people, HELP people, BUILD people, FORGIVE people, and SHARE with people, while exhibiting outright humility, compassion, and integrity, we become usable by default with our flaws and all.

Self-satisfaction without sincere compassion for others will cause all that we do, say, and become to feel as if it is all in vain. Why do we sometimes feel that way? Most often, we feel that way because selfishness has crept into our lives. *"The Guarded Psalms of Prayer"* says that selfishness comes into our lives to steal our inner joy and peace with a superficial façade of Me, Me, Me. If one does not believe that, simply listen to the conversations of others, if the conversation is comprised of me, me, me, and not we, they, them, us, and our.....then we have our answer! Selfish, selfish, selfish!

Life is not about one person; it is about US....God uses one to help one....God uses one to help another....God uses us to keep the Law of Reciprocity going. Once we begin to forget about the reason why we are here or why we are doing what we do, we will find that we will begin to start exhibiting self-defiant behaviors that will cause one to become a victim of circumstance. *"The Guarded Psalms of Prayer"* says that too many incidents of victimization will cause the best of us to give up on people, to give up on ourselves, and most of all, to secretly give up on God as if it was His fault.

Prayer

Father, my God, in the Name of Jesus, draw close to me, for I am alone in Your presence, trusting You to fill my void from within. It is through You, O' Lord, that provisions will be made to soothe my weary soul. It is through You that I will survive the tricks of those who will try to prey on my vulnerability. It is through You that I am able to deal with the enemy inside of me.

As the deep calleth unto the deep, I am admitting to the fact that loneliness is creeping up into the depths of my soul, crippling my ability to move outside of my comfort zone. For that reason, my Comforter and Way Maker, I am asking that You step-in to provide all of my needs according to Your riches and glory. Just as I know that the scraps of companionship fall from the table to feed the dogs. How much more do You value me to have companionship of those who are my equal? In the Name of my Loving Savior, as I avail myself to companionship, I am invoking an overflow of equally yoked individuals, who are designed to help propel me, and not hold me back from that in which You have destined for me.

My Father, the Lover of my soul, as You provide more than enough love in my life, give me the ability to share it as well; therefore, providing a positive impact that can only come from You. By doing so, let me not hang my head down in shame, regarding my wants, needs, and desires to love and be loved by those who truly care about my well-being. Therefore, I invoke Divine Authority over my life to align my wants, needs, and desires with Your will and Your way; as my inner-born instinctual nature comes forth to bring healing and confidence in the choices that I am making or will make, in the Name of Jesus.

For You, O' Lord, it is my reasonable service to begin to walk by faith and not by sight. Although, people may look down on me for doing so—I am making it my business to look up to You, from whence my strength cometh. My Father, You are truly my help in my time of need; even though, I am being judged for being alone, but in Your presence, I have learned that I am never alone if I trust in You, as well as Your timing. And, by doing so, I command that the spirit of loneliness, depart into the pits of Hell, from whence it came. By Divine Decree, I am now the lender, and not the borrower of love or companionship. In the Name of Jesus. Thank you. Amen.

Scripture Reading:

Psalms 20

Psalms 26

Psalms 45

Psalms 47

Psalms 71

Psalms 119

Psalms 135

CHAPTER 15

Best Life of Psalms

If you want to begin to reap the benefits of *"The Guarded Psalms of Prayer"* you must begin to find a way to stop groaning, whining, and complaining about what people did not do for you, what people did to you, who did not love you, who hurt you, or how people treated you; because, if you are reading this book right now, it does not matter anyway! As a matter of fact, you are designed to R.O.A.R. after you become Mentally Free. Our R.O.A.R depends upon our ability to Respect ourselves and others, our ability to Overcome our challenges, our ability to Achieve the desires of our heart, and our ability to Reach back to help someone else. Is it that simple? Maybe or maybe not—it takes a certain developed mindset to R.O.A.R. on a level where you can be heard without having to say one word.

Now that you understand that you are free, now that you understand the rules of your soul, now that you understand that you are required to love, now that you understand how to pray, and now that you understand the repercussions of not doing the right thing….it is time for me to introduce *"The Guarded Psalms of Prayer"* on a mentally and emotionally mature level.

We are a compilation of what we believe….if we believe that we are lovable, then we are. If we believe that we are not, then we attract people into our lives that will treat us parallel to what we believe about ourselves. We are a magnet of our belief system; regardless of the façade that we put on….the inner magnet from within has a duty to call forth its representatives. But let me say this, on the negative side of things, our mind has a way of creating our very own perceptional images that will feed us back whatever we are thinking or believing, making it seemingly real; when it's our mind really playing tricks on us. Therefore, we must be careful about the self-talk that we are feeding ourselves on a moment-by-moment basis. *"The Guarded Psalms of Prayer"* says that we must get the facts before we allow our minds to run wild with untruths, our perception of things, our guiltiness, or our insecurities.

Now, on the positive side of things, it is our belief system that helps feed our integrity, our character, our instincts, and our know-how….If we have a belief system of a wise person, it's going to feed us wisdom along with a wise mentality. If we have a belief system of a successful person, it's going to feed us successful ideas, concepts, and precepts. If we have a belief system of a junkyard dog, it's going to feed us a doggy-dog mentality or a street mentality. If we have a belief system of a THOT mentality, it's going to feed us with THOT like behaviors and mentality; and the list goes on.

Now that we have that out the way, our lovability is a magnet as well—people can feel the love or the lack of it before we open our mouth. And, once we speak, it is the icing on the cake, the confirmation of an inner feeling or the confirmation of a repellant. A loving and caring personality can melt the heart of many, especially children. Believe it or not, children are the first to weed out fake, hateful, cruel, and wayward people. Children follow their instincts on lovability more than adults because we are trained to mask our feelings, but children are not well-developed in that particular area—so, if they reject people when first meeting them, exercise extreme CAUTION.

It is our belief that provides us with the motivation or provides us with an obstacle to satisfy what we are subconsciously envisioning. If we have a desire to enable our belief system to begin to work in our favor, we must learn how to become resourceful, positive, and change how we are viewing the people, places, and things in our lives, leaving no stone unturned. Once this is accomplished, this will become the fuel that gives us the ability to persevere through all obstacles in the Spirit of Love and Fluidity. *"The Guarded Psalms of Prayer"* says that when we learn how to acknowledge and apply the Power of Love in our daily lives, it will cause us to become a bed of resourcefulness that will draw greatness toward us. For me, it opened the door to Divine Guidance to share with those who are in need of what I have to offer.

If we believe that God is a living God, we should not wait until our back is up against the wall to seek His Hand—there is no need to ignore Him or disobey Him, He is just one belief away. Because of His love for us, He is ready, willing, and able to help adjust the way in which we are thinking, acting, or becoming. Trust me, the freedom from worry, fear, and anxiety brings about a peace that supersedes human understanding when we simply incorporate Him into our belief system. Plus, if He is the Source of everything anyway—it's only smart to trust that He will become our help in our time of need before we actually need "IT." *"For God will not withhold no good thing from those who walk uprightly."* Psalms 84:11.

The Rep

Our reputation and self-image are very important factors in living a life of greatness. Yes, perception is one thing; however, how we perceive ourselves is another. The power of the invisible is stronger than we think. Thoughts are invisible, yet powerful enough to bring an

Chapter 15 | Madam Oracle

idea into reality. Electricity is invisible, yet powerful enough to send a surge through our bodies. Love is invisible, yet powerful enough to make an unlovable person, lovable. Pain is invisible, yet powerful enough to make a strong person weak. The best way to attract the invisible is to simply read our goals daily, evaluate them weekly, and pray for Divine Guidance. This will enable us to become effective in our ability to become and stay focused while our intuition goes to work for us. It is our faith that will attract that one idea, that one thought, that one reaction, that one whatever…. that could change our lives forever.

"The Guarded Psalms of Prayer" says that when we are sincerely focused on what we need to do, we must not allow the left hand to know what the right hand is doing. Why reveal our dreams, desires, and hopes to those who will not provide a benefit to us. Actually, this is where the dream-killers come into play. There are certain dreams, hopes, desires and aspirations that we need to keep to ourselves until it's done. I firmly believe that we accomplish more when we talk less and do more! *"The Guarded Psalms of Prayer"* says that when we get caught up in talking about the shoulda, coulda, and woulda in life— we take time away from doing, accomplishing, and becoming. Less is more, especially when it comes down to giving out too much information.

The Trump Card

"*The Guarded Psalms of Prayer*" says that true power of who we are, is wrapped up in our ability to humbly pray. Prayer has been the most powerful key to my survival, not just in the bad times or in my moments of desperation, but in the good times as well. It has been a great tool that has changed my life tremendously. I thank God for the power of prayer and my ability to share this information with you; therefore, giving you the same ability to R.O.A.R on a level that supernatural in nature.

The 2nd Trump Card

"*The Guarded Psalms of Prayer*" says that meditation is one vital ingredient in life that most of us are missing. Actually, prayer is our way of talking to God and meditation is our way of listening to God as we review, purge, and manifest what we want and do not want in our lives. Often enough, the thought of sitting still, creates more unrest than the process of meditation itself. Meditation is a process of thinking, pondering, and releasing. This process gives us the ability to think through what we are doing, why we are doing, how we are doing, when we are doing, and where we are doing.

Meditation allows our inner man to speak, giving us the ability to understand our true greatness and the unlimited potential that we possess from within. When our outer man wants to dominate, we must determine whether our success is going to last, whether our peace is going to last, whether our mental stability is going to last, whether our lovability is going to last, etc. The stress of it all, will cause the best of us to create self-sabotage or to create booby-traps in other areas of our lives; and most often, it shows up in our bodies or in our love life.

Although, there are many different forms of meditation; however, I want you to develop your own form of meditation that works just for you. *"The Guarded Psalms of Prayer"* says that in order to truly master a particular area of your life, you will need to master the ability to follow the inner guide from within through the process of meditation, but not limited to meditation only. The empire that you truly desire from within, must be built in your mind before it makes its way to reality. Everything you have, do, or become will be formed as a thought first.

The 3rd Trump Card

"The Guarded Psalms of Prayer" says that you are like a sponge, soaking up everything around you, positively or negatively. If you want to feel better, look better, think better, or treat yourself/others better—GO EXERCISE; especially, when you feel a stress attack coming to invade your sanity. Most people use exercise to lose weight; as of today, you will now use exercise to lose stress. Get creative with your exercising; it does not have to be boring; frankly, walking is one of the best forms of exercise, so why not combine that with prayer,

and call it walking meditation as you grow toward your greatness.

Grow Great

"The Guarded Psalms of Prayer" says that personal growth compiled with spiritual growth gives you the option, as well as the opportunity to excel in everything that you do. It's amazing that when you believe that you have something valuable to offer others, the "HOW TO" develops! Just remember that God will meet you at the level of your expectation; especially when you are willing and dedicated to work together with others to produce something positive. *"The Guarded Psalms of Prayer"* also says that we are able to overcome or work through any type of obstacle, if we learn how to become humble enough to set goals, work on them, believe in ourselves, pray, fast, and meditate, while others talk, yearn, and waste time.

When you have a plan or roadmap to follow, no matter what happens in your life, you can always get back on track, no matter what! For that reason, *"The Guarded Psalms of Prayer"* has **99** Principles that you can live by:

1. Know that you must give each day back to God.
2. Know that you must pray and place God first in your life.

3. Know that you must prioritize God, self, spouse, children, and then others as a part of the Divine Order.

4. Know that no one can take your power from you unless you choose to give it away.

5. Know that happiness is a choice that you choose on a moment-by-moment basis.

6. Know that you are a gift from God, and resentment cannot steal your blessings from you, unless you give in to it.

7. Know that FEAR cannot stop the blessings God has for you. Always know that your blessing is on the other side of what you fear—Push through it!

8. Know that your gift will make room for you, and it will set you before men in high places.

9. Know that you are blessed to do what you do, and guilt has no place in your life.

10. Know that favor will open doors of opportunity for you.

11. Know that you must be willing to make the necessary sacrifices.

12. Know that a good name is chosen, and you must lead by example.

13. Know that you must accept responsibility for your actions and reactions.

14. Know that God can equip you, use you, and teach you what you need to know.

15. Know that risks are necessary for the challenges that will come your way.
16. Know that fault-finding is not conducive to where you are going in life.
17. Know that you must share and take action when necessary.
18. Know that communication is mandatory to achieve the desires of your heart.
19. Know that you do not have to entertain negative people, places, and things.
20. Know that mistakes and failures are just stepping stones designed to get you to the next level.
21. Know that you must encourage, inspire, and motivate others regardless of what you are going through.
22. Know that you must be willing to celebrate what God has done for you and through you to show your appreciation for His divine grace and mercy.
23. Know the value of seed, time, and harvest.
24. Know that you must be willing to love and serve others.
25. Know the Law of Reciprocity as well as the Law of Cause and Effect.
26. Know that God has your back when nobody else will.
27. Know that LOVE is written on the tablet of your heart.
28. Know that you must follow-through to develop discipline.

29. Know that you have the POWER to change your thoughts at any given time.
30. Know that you have the choice to expel negativity out of your life.
31. Know that you cannot blame others for your situation, actions, or experiences.
32. Know that God loves a cheerful, humble, and faithful servant.
33. Know that wisdom requires you to think before you speak.
34. Know that kind words will turn away wrath, allowing you to get your point across.
35. Know that when you communicate, you must look into the eyes of the person that you are speaking to.
36. Know that you should never give your power away by not assuming responsibility for your actions, reactions, thoughts, and conversations.
37. Know that every lesson in life is WISDOM for you to share.
38. Know that your past has no power over you if you use it as a TOOL to build your life or the lives of others.
39. Know that you are good enough for the gift that God has placed inside of you. You are the Best Y.O.U. that you have.
40. Know that you must be quick to forgive and move on to free your mind of unwanted clutter.

41. Know that you do not have to tolerate poor behavior, excuse yourself nicely.
42. Know that confrontation is not necessary when it's so easy to walk away as the bigger person.
43. Know that if anger is sparked in a conversation, you must become silent until a level of peace is established; if not, excuse yourself.
44. Know that your character is on the line every time you open your mouth.
45. Know that your reputation is your lifeline, it's not what people think about you—it's what you think about you that count! Hold fast to your integrity.
46. Know that when your conscience becomes your guide, you are able to truly live in peace with yourself.
47. Know that the past cannot hold you back if you release it.
48. Know that forgiveness is the TRUMP CARD you pull when you have gotten a bad deal; therefore, giving you the grace and mercy to heal, letting go without hating!
49. Know that you can overcome any obstacle because God will not place more on you than you can tolerate.
50. Know that you have the ability to create a win-win situation out of anything.
51. Know that you are here to inspire others.
52. Know that you must positively affirm everyone, even if you are smarter or wiser than they are—

you must always appear humble. Arrogance is a forbidden character trait for where you are going!

53. Know that you treat your enemies with kindness even when they betray you. Just keep your distance with a smile on your face and love them anyway.

54. Know that it is better to say less and do more.

55. Know that you must live every day like it is your last day, taking nothing for granted.

56. Know that you must smile even when you do not have anything to smile about—it is medicine for the soul.

57. Know that you must focus on your goals in life and not your obstacles.

58. Know that you must look for the good in all things, even when it does not appear to be there.

59. Know that you must leave no stone unturned. You must exhaust all of your resources.

60. Know that you cannot allow anyone to push your emotional trigger buttons unless they are positive.

61. Know that you must always expect the unexpected, so that you are never disappointed. Life happens, and you can always keep a smile on your face if you remove the expectations off of people, and place them on yourself. However, you would never tell them of course!

62. Know that you are a GENIUS at something, and it is up to you to find out what it is. You do not

have to do everything well, simply focus on doing a few things well and MASTER IT!

63. Know that you must learn how to let go and not stress out.

64. Know that you cannot solve every problem; you can only do your part.

65. Know that you have to relax and not respond to everything.

66. Know that you cannot overthink issues.

67. Know that procrastination is disguised as the fear of failure or confusion that needs to be dealt with immediately.

68. Know that you have a choice of which direction you take in life.

69. Know that when you determine your values and standards, it is much easier to determine your purpose.

70. Know that you cannot wander aimlessly expecting to achieve greatness.

71. Know that complaining is not an attribute that's conducive to positive living.

72. Know that when you judge others out of jealousy or envy, you bring judgment back to your own house; therefore, speak the truth in love.

73. Know that when you have your plan in writing, it seals the deal with the Universe.

74. Know that life becomes easier when you know what you want, when you have it in writing, when

you have it in your heart, and when you do not deviate from the plan.

75. Know that you have to pay attention to what life is trying to say to you.

76. Know that you must learn something new every day to keep your mind fresh.

77. Know that it is always good to lend a helping hand, expecting nothing in return.

78. Know that it is always good to respect your elders.

79. Know that the best leaders are the best followers and vice-versa.

80. Know that you must be on your best behavior at all times.

81. Know that it is best to always wish people well.

82. Know that you must be grateful for all things.

83. Know that you cannot be afraid to say what's on your mind or ask for what you want.

84. Know that whatever you desire, pay it forward to activate the Law of Reciprocity.

85. Know that you must give your mind time to think in total silence.

86. Know that you say "please" and "thank-you" to people.

87. Know that you must be prompt; it is not good to be late.

88. Know that there is no need to be rude to anyone—always offer compassion to everyone, even if they do not deserve it.

89. Know that you must exercise self-respect in every area of your life.
90. Know that you must venture out of your comfort zone.
91. Know that you must multi-task in order to get things accomplished from time-to-time.
92. Know that you may have to think outside, inside, around, and through the box in order to get what you want.
93. Know that you have to follow your instincts.
94. Know that you cannot make excuses for your mishaps in life.
95. Know that you must remain true to thyself.
96. Know that your little becomes much when you appreciate it and place it in the Hands of the Lord.
97. Know that with every "no" you are that much closer to a "yes."
98. Know that you will have better results in life when you pray about permanent decisions before you make them.
99. Know that if you need a little courage on your journey, simply take a big R.O.A.R.! Trust me, it works.

"The Guarded Psalms of Prayer" says that filling the needs of others can and will open the door to getting our own personal needs, wants, or desires met. When we open our hands first out of the goodness of our heart, that

enables God to open His hands: As Scripture concurs, *"Give, and it will be given to you: good measure, pressed down, shaken together, and running over will be put into your bosom. For with the same measure that you use, it will be measured back to you."* Luke 6:38.

"The Guarded Psalms of Prayer" says that when we begin to secretly lose hope, we will begin to lose our substance regarding what we will stand for or what we will stand under; therefore, becoming the culprit of our compromises. The first sign of hopelessness is when we find ourselves expecting others to do for us what we are not willing to do for ourselves.

It behooves me how we expect others to believe in us, but we do not believe in ourselves. As a matter of fact, we want others to think that we are beautiful, but we do not believe that we are; we want someone to give to us, but we are ungrateful, selfish, and taking more than we give back. Now, this takes the cake; we desire for someone to love us, but we are not loving, or we are cruel in our actions, reactions, and/or attitude! We want someone to show kindness, but we ourselves are very rude......what a contradiction!

"The Guarded Psalms of Prayer" says that secretly or silently losing hope in ourselves will cause us to live by double standards. Hopelessness leads to false expectations, false expectations lead to disappointment, and too many disappointments will lead to self-sabotage. Think about it! Hope has more power than we

give it. Today, it is your time to regain your hope from within and be the great person that you are by simply allowing the Fruits of the Spirit into your life. I promise you that you cannot go wrong exercising love, joy, peace, mercy, kindness, goodness, faithfulness, gentleness, and self-control. You deserve the best, so believe that you are the best at what you are gifted to do, say, and become.

"The Guarded Psalms of Prayer" says that you are FREE. You are the R.O.A.R. that keeps on roaring....you are the KING of your territory, you are the King of your pride, you are the King over your mind, and most of all, you are the King over your perception. You can achieve anything that you so desire, if you learn how to R.O.A.R. with Godly Character that resides within the depth of your soul. To serve and be served inside and outside of your Kingship with love, kindness, and compassion are SUPREME. So, go ahead and let your R.O.A.R. shine; be blessed and be a blessing to someone else.

Prayer

Examine me, O' LORD, and try me; test my mind and my heart as You search my hidden motives, making them pure as gold. I pray for favor, health, wealth, and good success over my life, my finances, my family, my job, and all those I come in contact with. Allow the Love of Christ to flow through my veins, giving me the

Breath of Life to empower and inspire myself, as well as those around me. I am praying for unity and wholeness from within the depths of my loins to bring forth Your will and Your way in my life. For I am seeking You with all my heart as I use my body as a Living Sacrifice that is holy and acceptable unto You. As I invoke Your presence in this phase of my humility, I am asking that You lead me to a place that's higher than this fleshly realm of life.

Father, my God, in the Name of Jesus, over the next 40 days, I declare and decree that You reveal ideas, concepts, strategies, and wisdom that will propel me into my destiny of greatness. As I give You the full range of freedom to operate in and around my life, I will not take anything for granted. I am calling forth my inner wisdom along with the grace and mercy that You have on my soul to give me the fuel needed for this journey. The anointing that You have placed within me is on assignment to help me to accomplish that in which You want and desire in my life. For that reason, I command the fear of the known or unknown to release its grip on my life; therefore, infusing me with Divine Favor that's beyond all human understanding.

As I embark upon this journey, the things of old, and the mistakes that I have made in the past doesn't matter anymore—I am moving forward with a clean slate of greatness that will have an impact on generations to come. From this day forward, when I look within myself, I accept total responsibility for my life; while breaking the yolk of all the negative people, places, and things that are in it. By divine decree, I am embracing spiritual abundance from the inside out; therefore, I call forth my blessings from the North, South, East, and West.

Today, remove any poverty-stricken ideologies from my path as I move forward into supernatural abundance, bringing forth the MENTAL GENIUS that is hidden inside of me. It is written that You are the Source to all of my wealth, ideas, strategies, and concepts; therefore, I am laying claim to my inheritance. Father, as I am esteemed in Your sight, my mind is abounding in Your everlasting greatness as I embrace the love, peace, and prosperity that rightfully belongs to me. In the Name of Jesus. Amen. Thank you.

Scripture Reading:

Psalms 14
Psalms 19
Psalms 84
Psalms 94

Madam Oracle

The Blessing Prayer

Father, My God, in the Name of Jesus, I humbly come before You with a meek heart, as an ambassador of Christ seeking reconciliation with You. If I have found favor in Your sight, let everyone see the signs of Your goodness, grace, and mercy. As a wonderful Way Maker to all, I know that no weapon formed against me will prosper without just cause; nor, do I even want to form a weapon against myself by sowing intentional or unintentional unrighteousness to sabotage my favor.

As a weapon of warfare in Christ Jesus, I know that the level of my favor is governed by the intents of my heart; therefore, on this day, I pray for cleanliness from my innermost being. Vindicate me Lord, as I seek Your face with all my heart—cleanse me from my daily debris that I have unawaringly picked up. I trust You to clean my filthy dirty rags of my past, present, and future, to include my ungodly thoughts and my harbored unforgiveness, to ensure that my wisdom comes from You, and not the emotional critic from within. My God, during this cleansing process, I know that when Your voice is silent, it means that you are working things out in my favor. And, all I need to do is to exercise my faith as You reveal the evidence of things I hoped for.

As a Child of the Most High, let the Spirit of the Peacemaker come forth right now, in the Name of Jesus. For, it is through You, along with Your grace and mercy that my gift will allow me to speak life into myself and others as well. Lord, as I hunger and thirst for Your righteousness, let Your favor cover every area of my life, to ensure that I will then be able to allow Your favor to permeate through me into the lives of others. My confidence resides within You, my Heavenly Father, as You guide, protect, and anoint me in Your Will, as well as Your Way of living a fruitful, productive life of Your bestowed favor.

My God, with clean hands, pure heart, and sober mind, open up the windows of Heaven and pour me out a blessing that I will not have room enough to store. For it is You that my hope rests in, it is You that my strength cometh, it is You that my help cometh from, it is You O'Lord, it is You. For this divine favor, O' Lord, I give thanks to You, while Your praises continually flow from my lips. Thank you. Amen.

The Blessing Prayer | Madam Oracle

THE GUARDED WISDOM OF PSALMS
Psalm Index

Purpose	Psalm
Abundance	23
Aligning Your Thoughts	71
Anger	73
Anointing Home	108
Answers From God	141
Anxiety	31
Anxiety	12
Anxiety	13
Appreciation For Blessings	30
Assistance From God Daily	132
Assuming Responsibility	82
Assurance In Time Of Need	99
Attacks	28
Attitude Of Gratitude	66
Attract Good Business	8
Attract Greatness	84
Awareness	95
Bad Habits	69
Bad Influences	68
Bad Memories	105
Balance	52
Battle	20
Be Anxious For Nothing	55
Bearing A Heavy Load	145
Bedtime Prayer	4

Financial Help	72
Find Yourself	44
Flourish	132
Flourish	115
Forgiveness	85
Forgiveness	15
Forgiveness	25
Forgiveness	75
Forgiveness	103
Forgiveness	119
Friendliness	67
Friendliness	133
Frustrated	40
Frustrated With Life	40
Fulfillment	111
Future Plans	84
Gain Power	130
Gateway To A Higher Self	23
Get Rid Of Pride	131
Giving Thanks	65
Good Energy	123
Good Fortune	74
Good Life	16
Good Ventures	112
Gossip	12
Grace	36
Grace	103
Gratefulness	66
Gratefulness	65
Gratefulness	150

Restore Faith	77
Restore Faith	143
Rivalry Favor	127
Roadblocks	10
Rumors	12
Safe Drive	28
Safe Journey	124
Safe Travels	121
Safeguard Thoughts	24
Safety	4
Save From A Battle	20
Scandal	31
Secret Enemies	64
Seeking A Specific Answer	102
Seeking Mercy For Sin	85
Self-Pity	117
Serenity	31
Serenity	23
Serenity	108
Sins	85
Sleeping	4
Smiling Therapy	48
Snares Of The Enemy	11
Sociability	67
Spiritual Awakening	5
Spiritual Battle	7
Spiritual Blessings	21
Spiritual Cleanse	29
Spiritual Covering	31
Spiritual Desire	134

Printed in Great Britain
by Amazon